LIVE YOUR TRUTH

LIVE YOUR TRUTH

START YOUR JOURNEY
TO FREEDOM AND HEALING

COLLEEN GALLAGHER

NEW YORK

LONDON • NASHVILLE • MELBOURNE • VANCOUVER

LIVE YOUR TRUTH

START YOUR JOURNEY TO FREEDOM AND HEALING

Published in New York, New York, by Morgan James Publishing. Morgan James is a trademark of Morgan James, LLC. www.MorganJamesPublishing.com

Morgan James BOGO™

A **FREE** ebook edition is available for you or a friend with the purchase of this print book.

CLEARLY SIGN YOUR NAME ABOVE

Instructions to claim your free ebook edition:
1. Visit MorganJamesBOGO.com
2. Sign your name CLEARLY in the space above
3. Complete the form and submit a photo of this entire page
4. You or your friend can download the ebook to your preferred device

ISBN 9781631955860 paperback
ISBN 9781631955877 ebook
Library of Congress Control Number: 2021935609

Cover Design by:
Ana Grigoriu-Voicu

Interior Design by:
Chris Treccani
www.3dogcreative.net

Morgan James is a proud partner of Habitat for Humanity Peninsula and Greater Williamsburg. Partners in building since 2006.

Get involved today! Visit
MorganJamesPublishing.com/giving-back

ACKNOWLEDGMENTS

To all of those out there who live with our heart,
this is our time.
This is our movement.

To parents, friends and to the world,
thank you for inspiring, empowering and
impacting me to give this out in the world.

TABLE OF CONTENTS

WELCOME

Thank you for picking up this book. As you hold it in your hands, I am sending you a huge Colleen squeeze full of love and positivity! I am inviting you on a journey with me. A journey where we learn to live as one in the world, become Intoxicators, and create a better world for all of us.

The Intoxicator Movement is for those of us with the bold, imaginative hearts and minds, the wanderlust and those of us who hold the beautiful desire within to dream of a world where love is the way. But most us dreamers, visionaries and wanders have given up because of all the negativity that surrounds us in the world. This is for those of us who are living these two separate lives because we have lost hope of the dream, vision, and fairytale idea to live in a world where love will always prevail. We are at war within ourselves and the world because we think love has been defeated.

So, what does it mean to become an Intoxicator?

I hear that question so often. Yet my real question is: How do you live every day of your life *not* intoxicating the world with your truth? Being an Intoxicator is when you take time to create space to look within, remove the toxic, and become what's left— your truth in the world.

But, I get it. To imagine we can live in a world where every person is given the equal opportunity to live their truth seems impossible, right?

To live every day openly acknowledging who you truly are.

To live every day discovering all the possibilities to just be yourself.

To live every day exploring your true self in the world.

To live every day authentically loving who you are.

To live every day intoxicating the world with who you are; that seems weird, right?

To live in a world of people sharing vulnerabilities, authentic emotions, and who we truly are seems far too idealistic.

That's what I thought for nine long years! After nine years of isolating myself, and causing self-suffering, I took the time to envision a world where each person was living their truth and how magical that would be.

I started with my own life and began living my truth. Then from my vision, I crafted The Intoxicator Movement. With it I want to inspire, empower, and impact you to live every single day with your truth, so that when your final day comes, you can truly say you have no regrets.

This is the beginning of our journey. The journey to become Intoxicators, to courageously live our truth, and to contribute to making this world a better place for each of us!

INTRODUCTION

I n this book, I will share with you how I was defeated by the world for nine long years. I lost the dreamer who lives inside of me, the one who knew the fairytale could still come true. In this book I share how, I finally overcame the harsh realities of the world and made this movement come alive. As we start our journey together, we are becoming united, joining our energy together to create momentum to prove our truth that love will always prevail.

In this journey I take you through a story of a few of my life experiences that led me to suppress my truth and carry many subconscious behaviors, habits, and thoughts where I remained a victim to the world. At age 23, I had a shift and crafted this vision into movement. I'm passionate about sharing what I've learned because the world has impacted me to become aware that many of us live our entire lives subconsciously carrying various negative behaviors, habits, and thought patterns that limit our true potential. With this vision, book, and movement, it is my hope that no one will ever feel they need to isolate them-selves from the world again.

I was born in Detroit, Michigan, where I had a very normal upbringing. I am an only child and was born to two caring, driven, and selfless parents who are very in love! At the time of writing this book, I have lived in seven cities, two countries, visited 31 countries, and visited 28 of the 50 states in the United States. I have met people from all over the world, experienced life, and learned to live.

I went to Michigan State University where I graduated with a Bachelor of Arts in Marketing. I was President of my busi-ness organization and did three study abroads: in Cuba, the United Kingdom, and South Africa. I had paid internships every summer and even got to live in Arizona for one of the summers! After I graduated, I got a job and lived in Texas, then moved to Maryland. At age 23, I quit my job and moved to New Zealand. Looking in from the outside, it seems like I led a pretty success-ful, normal life, right?

Well, except at age 14 I was diagnosed with thyroid cancer.

I held onto my story of cancer until I was 23 years old. At age 23, I went to war with the world because I could not take it one moment longer feeling alone, feeling rejected for living my truth, and living in fear that love will not always prevail. I created The Intoxicator Movement so no one would ever again would need to feel alone, unworthy, unloved, or rejected again. I created this movement so we can empower each other to come together to stand up to the world by courageously living our truth with our tribe, to no longer feel defeated by the negativity and hate within the world. This book and movement is here so we can finally conquer the world together by transforming it with love.

The Intoxicator Movement is a five-step process where we create space for ourselves to look within, remove the toxic, and become what is left: our truest self in the world. An Intoxicator can be anyone—a home builder, gardener, hairdresser, CEO of corporate, stay-at-home mom or dad, the list can go on—but the common factor is we are the people in the world craving to live authentically. We are the ones who want to live with our hearts. We are the ones deep down who want to become part of the momentum of moving the world forward.

As an Intoxicator, we take our power back from the world and design our own personal roadmap for our fairytale dream to become reality.

My intention is to create a connection between us, inspiring and empowering each of us to begin to acknowledge the amazing power we hold within, allowing us to realize how similar we are. I want us to see the possibilities that exist for each of us. We can let go of trying to be what the world has molded us to be.

We each have fairytale dreams that we have pushed to the side because we thought there was no possible way our dreams could come true. This story I am about to share is truly our story, because it will show you how we have all experienced life-shaping events that have discouraged us and held us back from living our dreams. No matter what form your life-shaping event took, we all have that one life-shaping event. Even though person to person it is different, these events are the birth of our connection because it's the one thing we all have in common: a struggle that we have had to overcome. With this story I hope to inspire, empower, and impact you so, you can see the possibility that your dream can come alive too.

My mission with this movement is to inspire, empower, and impact one billion people to start living their truth courageously, by becoming Intoxicators, so that that each person this movement touches will live a life with no regrets.

THE CANCER

I remember that Tuesday as the "normal" 14-year-old Colleen. I was a sophomore in high school. I was at basketball practice wearing a red jersey, going for a layup when I collapsed. Suddenly, I was gasping for air and was taken to the emergency room. I was quickly told that my thyroid was enlarged and I would need surgery as soon as possible. They said after I had this surgery I would be on medication for the rest of my life, and when I wanted to have a family, I would need to go to the doctors to get my medication adjusted.

My first surgery came and went, but then there was a lymph node with cancer cells that managed to get tangled with my jugular vein. I had to have another surgery within two months of the first one. This second surgery was going to be a higher risk and longer surgery. Surgery number two came and went; I survived, completely clear of new cancer diagnoses at age 20. However, all the experiences that came from having cancer—going to numerous doctor visits, how various people react to cancer affecting them and their families, the realities of the USA health care system, having to be on medication every day starting at 14, and having a scar on my neck—is what I allowed to defeat me, I let this rob me of seeing the possibility to live my dreams. I thought I could only follow the traditional path to ensure I would always have money, healthcare and hopefully it would bring me the dream lifestyle, just like a real-life Disney movie.

At age 14 my life changed drastically within seconds. Usually, most people react: "You were so young." My real reaction at that time was, I am now ugly. I CANNOT leave the house because I have a scar on my neck! I did not even care about the cancer itself because at 14 years old I had no idea what that even meant. I was so consumed at how the world would look at me now that I had a scar and this disease, cancer attached to my name.

Like most 14-year-old girls, my self-esteem was not the highest in the world. I went to school the next day, and it seemed like everyone was asking why I was rushed to the hospital. Now I realize there were many people who did not ask anything about it, but at the time, 30-some-odd people questioning me seemed like the whole world. I didn't feel different, but I knew I had this word attached to me now and possibly something growing inside me. The last thing I wanted to tell people was that I would need surgery because I may have cancer.

I let this disease become a nine-year battle, even after it was no longer within me. I subconsciously carried the harsh realities I was exposed to with various people's reactions to when cancer affects them and their family. I carried survivor's guilt, feeling unworthy to be alive in my later teens when children younger than me were dying, and I chose to carry anger against the world. I felt helpless because it appeared we did not want to find a cure to cancer, it brings in too much money for the medical field. I lost hope in the world because I felt defeated. I thought I had no possibility to find a way in the world, to carve my own path, not having to follow the traditional path of chasing money and healthcare.

As I walk you through the subconscious anger, unworthiness, and guilt I carried around long after cancer was gone, I have become aware that many of us subconsciously carry these feelings within us. As I mentioned before, the world has given each of us a cancer or disease, just in various forms. This disease has impacted us equally, because we each have had to overcome struggles and that allows us to have an immediate connection with each other, because it's something we all have in common. I am using my cancer to empower The Intoxicator Movement, the movement of a lifetime, to have us come together as one, as a peaceful army to fight back, carving the path to empower love to become the truth of the world.

I hope within this adventure we are about to start, you can start to look within your heart to search for any small way you can stand up, fight back, and become an Intoxicator to bring the most love you have within you back into this world. Every small act of love contributes to empowering you to live a life with no regrets, and it impacts the world to become so filled with love that, hopefully one day, there will never be another one of us who dreams of a world filled with love, defeated, heartbroken, and acting in ways of subconscious anger, unworthiness, and guilt toward the world.

This book is our moment, this is our Movement, we are starting a peaceful army of love to fight back against the harsh realities of the world we have been exposed to. This is our time. We will show the world, together, united, as Intoxicators, those living our truth, we are finally going to conquer the world by transforming it with love.

THE SCAR

I went to high school with around one thousand kids, and immediately after the first surgery, it seemed like everyone and their family starting noticing me. They were curious about the scar on my neck and asked a lot of questions. Imagine being a teenager trying to explain to other kids that you were in and out of doctors' offices because you had cancer and now this is why you looked weird.

When this scar was born, I begged my parents to buy me more scarves and turtlenecks so I wouldn't have to explain at school why I had this weird scar on my neck. I bought tons of makeup to try to cover up my red scar. I was doing everything I could to hide this disease that was given to me. This scar brought all kinds of unwanted attention to me by other kids at school. I would always make up some excuse rather than admit it was cancer because I did not want it to be some huge dramatic thing. However, this is when the subconscious anger began to build within me as I started to hide who I really was from the world. I thought my scar made me ugly, and at that time I thought being attractive was the ultimate goal in life.

While I was still a teenager, I begged my Mom to let me get plastic surgery to remove it. My mom said, "You will need to leave it for a year, and if you still feel the same then, we'll talk about getting you surgery." My experience of not feeling beautiful, wanting to hide my life from the world, started at this point.

Cancer was the last thing I wanted to talk about. I did not understand cancer let alone want to tell people in high school that I had it. Boys and girls would ask me what was on my neck and make fun of my scar. I always tried to hide it, pretending this was not my life.

This was just the beginning. In the nine years I've had my scar, over 800 people have said rude things, commented about it, or asked if I'm okay. That's an average seven times a month or almost twice a week. It felt like a cloud following me around. The majority of the comments were in high school and my first three years at college. It did decrease significantly when I turned 21 and left college.

We all probably realize we've had hurtful things said to us. What we may not realize is that it's us who gives intense meaning to the rude and hurtful comments we receive.

This whole drama of not feeling beautiful in my own skin is how I started to hide my story and my truth from the world. I subconsciously locked myself in a very dark, isolated room. During these nine years there were four comments made to me by four separate people that were forever ingrained in my mind. I found it impossible to let go of these four comments until I created The Intoxicator Movement. I am hesitant to share these four comments because they carry such an intense negative energy, but it's important that I share them so you can see that we, at the individual level, have the power to give meaning to this world around us. These four comments brought us to share this moment together.

By sharing these comments, I want us to begin our journey of learning how we carry anger, guilt, and unworthiness within us without realizing it. As I said in the beginning of the book, these exact comments might not have been said to you, but I'm sure we have shared the same emotions felt when these comments were said to me. Here are the four comments:

- A boy in one of my high school classes said, "You are ugly because of your neck."
- Another random guy at high school asked in the hallway, "Did your black boyfriend cut you?"
- Some guy at a party in college asked, "Did some guy choke you out during sex?"
- A guy at a frat party asked, "Are you okay? Did you try to kill yourself?"

I still cringe when telling these stories because I don't want you to take only the bad things away from my story. But these four comments are so important to tell since they are the foundation for this movement. They are the reason I chose to remain a victim of my life, and they're also how I was finally able to see the possibility that with this movement I could inspire, empower, and impact people to change the world with love.

Cancer ended up being a gift for me; from it I found my true mission in the world, but it took me nearly a decade to fully understand it. I only realized cancer was a gift after I quit my successful job at age 23 and moved across the world from Baltimore, Maryland, to New Zealand.

I have always been obsessed with traveling since I was a little girl. It's always been like a real-life Disney movie for me to travel all over the world, but I wanted to live internationally to see what it was like to live somewhere else. I ended up choosing New Zealand because I had been to Europe a ton already, and I chose an English-speaking country because I was going to be stressed about not having a job. I looked at visa requirements for several countries, and New Zealand seemed to have it all. It was $20 for a one-year visa, and it is known for its beautiful landscapes. I hoped it would empower me to find myself. So off I went to New Zealand, following my dream of living internationally, with no friends or family around. It was the first time I saw the possibility I can live my truth on my own terms. While in New Zealand it was the first time I became open to seeing this story of mine had nothing to do with cancer.

In New Zealand, I was sitting at an HR recruiting firm, in a cube, getting interviewed by this amazing girl who was going to try and get me a job. I remember in that moment I looked out the window overlooking the Auckland bridge with all the sailboats around with this breath-taking scenery, and I realized it did not matter who I was, what I had accomplished, or anything about my past. In that moment everything shifted, I realized I was holding onto everything with cancer, those four comments, so I could remain a victim of my own life and not have to be responsible for my own self-created shitty reality.

As I mentioned the world gives each of us a disease, a few examples are divorce, family members dying, break-ups, addiction, eating disorders, being discriminated against, etc. It is important to understand we all have an equally traumatic experience or event that has happened to us; we each have suffered equally. This suffering is the one consistent thing across all of us no matter what walk of life we come from, we all have shared this pain. This book empowers us to see how we can join together to overcome our diseases the world has given us, and that we do not need to be so divided. The truth is we all want to just feel a bit more loved and accepted.

We will explore how we have traveled this journey together already. I will walk you through how my whole life has been connected to this moment—this moment of you turning the pages in this book—and I'll give you tools to look within and see how your own life is connected to this very moment. I will focus on how I subconsciously manipulated myself for nine freaking years (this sounds like forever to me), with the hope that it inspires you to find ways you may be doing this within your own life without realizing it.

With this book I want to paint a clear picture of how my vision for The Intoxicator Movement came to life. I put myself through hell in order to learn how to live my truth and become an Intoxicator. I crafted this vision into a movement so that people could see there is a choice. We do not have to suppress our truth or isolate ourselves from the world and suffer alone. For nine long years I thought I didn't have the option to live my truth with love. Now I have devoted my life to finding ways to inspire and empower every single person to find their truth and live it too.

When you live your truth, other people can see the power and momentum of you living your truth. Whenever one of us begins to live our truth, we create a ripple effect of joy and love that is felt by more people around us than we even realize. The momentum grows, and the world can't help but be a better place. Just imagine for a moment a world where we inspire ourselves and everyone around us to live our truest, best selves. It's amazing, right? We would start to change the world together.

I've dedicated myself to presenting my vision in a five-step process to fight back against the world.

But I can't do it alone. This movement needs you.

The Intoxicator Movement is made up of this five-step process. If you decide to become an Intoxicator, I promise you will become part of something greater. You will start to live your truth courageously, and at the end of your life, you will be able to say you've lived a life with no regrets.

STARTING OUR JOURNEY

I f you have gotten to this page, let's take a moment and cele-
brate together. CONGRATS! You made it through the awful
saga. I am so grateful you had the patience, determination, and
resilience to make it through the negativity in that story.

I am proud of you and grateful you got this far! I am excited
for our journey together and for the day I will get to meet you,
learn your name, and give you the BIGGEST Colleen squeeze.

My mind is now totally focused on you in this moment, and
I hope you can be totally focused on this content as well. So
where do we begin?

Let's take a minute and breathe together, wherever you are,
let's breathe!

If you think this is stupid, as I would have once thought too,
let's think about that negative thought. Taking a moment out
of your day to breathe; you think you are above that. Why? I
really want you to dig deep if you think breathing is stupid and
figure out why. The worst thing that could happen when you
consciously breathe is you might look silly and someone around

you might laugh. At least you're spreading positivity into the world!

Okay, let's begin. Take the biggest inhale, the one where your chest rises and you feel your tummy expanding. Then give a huge exhale! Exhale, releasing all of that internal energy back into the world. Let's do this three to five times. This is here to allow ourselves to create space for ourselves to be present in this moment.

AHHH…do you feel that energy within, breathing deeply like we just practiced? We deserve depth. We deserve to create space to treat ourselves with time to reflect, time to learn to love who we truly are, and time to realize what we hold within us. So often, without realizing it, we never even create space to take time for ourselves and for our body to just breathe deeply. We just breath as quickly as we can, so we can just move onto the next thing because we think we have all this stuff going on. Deep down, we all know the most meaningful things in life, are those times we created space and allowed things to grow. Now that we have created a space within us, we can focus our attention on what's in front of us: this book. In it I'll walk you through the steps of becoming an Intoxicator!

The five steps to becoming an Intoxicator:

1. Become Open
2. Discover
3. Explore
4. Love
5. Intoxicator

This book will take us on a journey through each of these five steps. I'll explain how the four hurtful comments that I let drag me down relate to the various steps. You will see how our life journey is very similar. Finally, my intention with this book is that you will know with certainty how to find your truth, and that when you do, you will be an Intoxicator in the universe instead of getting intoxicated with information overload by the world. You can live a life with no regrets!

STEP ONE

Become Open

Our journey starts with becoming open to seeking who we truly are and no longer suppressing our truth.

I look back now at my 14-year-old self when I was rushed to the hospital and found out I would need surgery and that I might have cancer. Within moments so much can change. The experiences that I was exposed to as a result of being diagnosed with cancer at age 14 was the turning point of my self-created downward spiral. At that age, I had no idea what surgeries really entailed, what having to be on medication for the rest of your life meant, or what the doctors meant when they told me I would need to talk to a doctor when I wanted to have kids. I didn't get why all of a sudden, I was being called ugly, teased, or given unwanted attention because of a scar on my neck.

I had no clue what meaning to attach to all of these events happening to me because inside I still felt normal. However, I began allowing the world to make me feel abnormal, and even though most teenage girls probably feel abnormal as well, I subconsciously began to crave ways to connect in the world but without connecting over my truth, because that was too painful to face.

I so badly wanted to erase cancer and what was happening to me. I was also afraid to tell people what was really going on in my life. From that day, I began to subconsciously close myself off from the world. I began to hide who I truly was from the world. Without realizing it, I alienated myself from all the other kids my age. I slowly stopped doing sports, I would create drama with my friends over the smallest things, which led to me hanging out with the wrong type of people, and I started to always be "busy."

Deep down, I was angry for being chosen to have cancer, angry to see how cancer was tearing families apart over money. I was angry that children younger than me were given cancer, and I felt guilty not every one of them were able to beat cancer like I had. I felt abnormal for having these feelings. I was afraid if I told other high schoolers about my life outside of school, I would be made fun of. I was afraid that I would be rejected because my life no longer seemed normal compared to the other kids my age.

I started my journey of creating connections with my friends over dating, drinking and drama to talk about this anger, guilt, loneliness and unworthiness I was experiencing. I started craving connections to release the intense feelings and experiences I was having. I began what I now call my dating hobby, going out all the time, and hanging out with anyone who would be my friend. I put myself around people and in places where I ended up feeling rejected, unloved, and lonely. I was in relationships where I would let myself be used. I had no boundaries of communication with what was going on in any friendship or relationship, and because of these unhealthy relationships I would end up feeling angry toward the world.

I began a journey to isolation because I felt all alone in the world, like no one out there could understand this darkness that was taking over me.

BIG SMALL MOMENTS

It seems like such a simple concept to become open to who you are, but take a moment right now to think about your life. The reality is your life is completely made up of a bunch of small moments.

Remember in the beginning of the book when we were breathing? I made us take a moment to create space and take a few deep breaths even if it meant someone around us might laugh. I mentioned that we deserve to create time to give ourselves space to just be. I touched on us not even being aware that we take short breaths because we do not actively think about our breathing. The same thing we do with breathing, not being actively aware of how our behavior or thoughts affects us, we do with many things in life, including our disease.

Breathing is a silly example, but the reality is we do this every day subconsciously without thinking about it. When we start to live a life filled with subconscious small moments, before you know it, we end up living a life that may or may not be true to who we are. If we do not actively choose to become aware of all the small moments, we are not being true to ourselves. That is when the subconscious unworthiness, anger, and guilt gain momentum to build up within.

In this first step, I ask you to become open to thinking about all the small moments down to what you wear, how you talk to yourself, how you talk to others, and the activities you engage in because you might subconsciously be creating a life filled with moments that are not true to you, because you think this is the only way, because the world has defeated you too.

As I have stated the world gives each of us a disease, and we are left with two options: we can choose to become open to what we are going through, or we can choose to hide it from the world and pretend it never happened. The majority of us go with the second option, without actively being aware that we do this. We suppress it and pretend it never happened.

Why do we do this?

Take a moment and think about it in regards to your own life. The answer is we do it because we think it's way easier to pretend this event never happened, so that the uncomfortable feelings will be numbed. It seems easier to resume our normal life because it seems too much to bear to look at ourselves and the world with love when this darkness has randomly come into our life. When we do this, suppressing or turning a blind eye to the darkness that has entered into our life, all we are accomplishing is starting our journey to isolation. From my short time on this earth I have realized, unfortunately, many of us walk through life in this dark room.

Another example of a small moment that is presented so many times within our life where we suppress our truth is when someone asks us, "How are you?" We usually reply with, "good" or "great."

We think it is much easier to pretend that we each never have problems. We think it's easier to walk through life acting as we always have this magnificent perfect life. We get so caught up in this idea of having the perfect life that if anything does not fit into that perfect image we just cannot deal with, we suppress it. This is exactly what we do with whatever our disease, we suppress it, hoping it will magically disappear. That it will never disrupt us, from looking like we lead this perfect life. We hope the struggle and pain will just go away so we will never have to deal with it emotionally.

This question, "How are you?" is a HUGE small moment because most of us get asked it every day. However, when we answer this small question repeatedly over time not responding with our truth, we are creating moments that are hiding ourselves from the world. Each time we are asked, "How are you?" we have a powerful opportunity to accept the world's invitation to express ourselves. If we decide not to become open to what we are feeling and just respond with "good" or "great" in these small daily moments, what will our life look like when the world invites us to express ourselves for the big moments?

Think about your life with the small moments of breathing, the activities you engage in, responding to "how are you?", and what clothes you have and LOVE. Become aware, because the lack of awareness of all the small moments we subconsciously find to hide our truth slowly leads to our very own, self-created, dark, isolated room that hinders the world. If we do not become open to these moments, we are not becoming open to seeing we have the possibility to look within and remove the toxic so we can live our truth to gain the ultimate goal with living a life with no regrets.

THE FIRST COMMENT

I will introduce the first out of the four comments as it relates to becoming open.

The first comment I remember clearly. I was in my fourth-hour science class, we were in the computer lab that day, and I was in the fourth row. This boy was one row in front of me to the left, and we were talking about something, and all of a sudden, he said,

"You are ugly because of your neck."

I responded, telling him to "Shut up."

The teacher then told me, "Don't be so sensitive."

I allowed this comment to bring me so many insecurities, along with an intense anger. Every time I saw this guy after this comment, I was so angry at him. I would glare at him or physically get angry. I carried this anger toward him for the rest of my time in high school.

I found out a few years after high school that this boy committed suicide. I remember finding out, and my heart dropped. In that moment, I realized this guy said that comment filled with negativity subconsciously for me to respond with anger. When we both were in this place of anger, we emotionally connected. This comment was said to me in anger and I reacted in anger because we both connected for a moment without having to show any vulnerability. We could leak our anger out of us into the world hoping some anger would come back to get a quick moment of emotional arousal to have a short lived instant connection. When I found out he committed suicide I realized this, and I realized so many of us, so often, subconsciously act in ways of anger to get this instant short-lived connection. We then get addicted to these instant short-lived connections, so we start to attract them all the time in our lives and then blame the world for being so awful. In my moment shared with that boy and in the moments we each allow this to happen in our lives we allow the world to conquer us.

This small comment allowed me to unleash the anger I was feeling for isolating myself by pretending cancer never happened to me. Instead of letting this small, superficial comment go, I decided to carry this story around with me without any resolution for myself. I used this comment to constantly think the world is all bad so I could remain a victim.

When we decide to pretend our traumatic experience or event never happened, and that everything is like it was before the event or experience, we subconsciously act in emotionally harmful ways toward ourselves, others around us, and the world. When we deny our trauma, we are denying ourselves the privilege to look at whatever happened to us in life with the understanding we will never be the same again. We think we are on the quickest road to healing ourselves, but we are actually on the quickest road to self-destruction, creating subconscious small habits that lead up to a complete lifestyle where we isolate ourselves from the world.

Nine years later, I became open to accepting that I created a wall between me and the world, thinking no one could possibly understand what I was feeling. I held onto this small comment in hopes he would react with anger. I craved that short-term instant connection. It was a release for both of us to connect and then blame the world for being awful, which deep down was us releasing our truth of feeling defeated by the world from our disease. I now realize the anger I carried from this comment and various other small comments I experienced was my subconscious trying to speak to me, trying to tell me I was the one creating the problem. ME. There was no one else initiating this anger, no one else bringing this comment up again. This was all ME making myself a victim of the world.

This first step in very difficult. I have walked us through one very intense example and through smaller moments where we subconsciously suppress our truth. We walk around the world not responding honestly to how we are truly doing each day, to this extreme example of holding onto anger from a comment said to me about my scar, which my disease gave me. We think it's better to connect for an instant than to understand how we could create a much deeper and greater connection.

When we are able to put ourselves in a position to finally become open, we create a space for ourselves. We create space to become self-aware and to see when and how we are acting in negative and harmful ways toward ourselves, others, and the world. When we become open, we are able to accept the traumatic events or experiences that occurred in our lives instead of suppressing them. When we become open, it is the first time we allow ourselves to look for the light switch in the dark room we have created.

INTEGRATION

I did not integrate cancer into who I was as a person, so it created nine years filled with a bunch of small moments of isolating myself from the world. I found many ways to subconsciously act with anger, negativity, and hate toward the world. I subconsciously did this in hopes of evoking anger, negativity, or hate to come back toward me to create an instant emotional connection so I could blame the world for being awful. This way I could reject the world, giving it no possibility to reject me. As I have walked through life exposed to various people affected by cancer or their unique disease, I have realized we each have done this and do this throughout our life.

A frequent example of this is when we get cut off by someone in traffic or we do not let someone go in front of us while we are waiting in traffic. We usually react with anger or frustration because those five seconds we just lost are *so* important. However, when the role is reversed and we cut someone off or we want to make a turn and no one will let us, we usually also respond with anger and say everyone is so selfish and the world is over. We always find a way to blame the world around us, because we subconsciously like to pretend we are not responsible for the world we create around us.

When we act this way, we are only doing it to cover up our true feelings from a bigger internal root issue we are too fearful to face. We decide to make it simple. We think it seems safer to walk around the world creating tons of instant connections, that only last for a short time, with little to no effort, where we don't have to show who we really are, because it protects us from being rejected over our truth. We subconsciously and sometimes consciously reject the world around us, hoping the world will reject us back, so we can get relief from a short-term, instant connection. We choose to suppress or numb our root issue because it's filled with too much pain, but when we do this we end up subconsciously putting that pain back into the world.

Think for a moment how deep this goes within our lives. Think of your life and how often you suppress things because you think that is what's best. We create a life living in fear of facing something too painful in order to create a world where we become the victim. We then feel it's okay to blame the world for being miserable. That's how we get to the point where our dreams seem too far away to reach and we feel defeated.

Truth be told, if we decided to look at what happened to us, acknowledge it was traumatic and that we may need some support, it would be too easy, right? It is far too hard to imagine that at least one person might have gone through something similar. Instead we think it is easier to pretend no one understands.

This is the beginning of denying ourselves the gift of looking within to acknowledge the ultimate, amazing power we have to overcome anything life throws at us. When these events happen, we have the power to become open to acknowledging and seeking the support we need to get through it. It is easier to reach out to the world and be open that what happened to you was traumatic. We do not need to hide from the world or pretend this event or experience never happened. Even after the negative experience, you are capable of being open to this "new" you and living a life full of love and light. You are able to take this experience, become open to it, and learn how to make it part of the who you are and live authentically.

For years, I used a variety of situations to find rejection in the world. I found all the ways to hide my true issues with anger, negativity, and hate in all types of small moments interacting with people. By doing this, I locked myself further and further away from healthy connections. Again, the only reason we act in harmful and angry ways toward ourselves, others, and the world is because it gives us the greatest chance to obtain an instant connection with the least amount of vulnerability having to be shown, so we think it decreases our chances of bring rejection. I chose to act this way because I thought it was the best outlet to release the intense feelings arising from cancer. I crafted this movement for us to see we are here for each other to become open to the harsh realities of the world, and that we can overcome it together.

This step of becoming open is only the beginning to our true self-sustaining and fulfilling journey in life. Nine years after getting cancer, I was exhausted waking up every day unhappy. I allowed myself to start looking back on the years with an openness to myself and what I had done. During those nine long years, I did not even realize I was being negative or that I was manipulating myself to hang around people and places where I would end up feeling rejected, lonely, and unloved.

Step one, becoming open, starts with awareness of the subconscious emotions we carry. The realization that we have the power to open ourselves to our truth in the small moments is the start of our journey. On this journey we can acknowledge who we are and forgive ourselves for suffering because we thought isolating ourselves was the only option. This is the hardest step because we have to commit to becoming open to who we are every single day, within every single moment.

ACKNOWLEDGE THE DISEASE

The day I became open to cancer was not until after I moved to New Zealand from Baltimore, Maryland. Seems crazy, right?

As I mentioned before I always had a dream to live internationally, I was only working in Corporate America because I thought that was my only option, to go international while still having healthcare and income. Well one day I had an epiphany, I was in my house in Baltimore after work, realizing I hated my job, I was putting myself in an emotionally abusive situation with this guy, I had no real friends around me because I was awful to be around and I was so unhappy. I had almost no purpose in my life besides waiting for the weekend so I could just lay in bed all day and go out at night. I remember it so clearly, I just had this long day at work, where something just didn't sit right anymore and when I got home I collapsed on my couch, I laid there sobbing, asking myself how did I get here, to this place of such darkness. Then I remembered, my dream to live internationally, I ran upstairs got my laptop, looked at visas and saw it was $20 for a one-year visa in New Zealand! I become open to the possibility I could live my dream on my own terms. I applied for my visa and got it within 24 hours! I figured what's the worst that could happen? It could not be worse than my current situation where I have surrounded myself with darkness. I saved for 3 months, then quit my job and off I went to hopefully fulfill my dream.

New Zealand was breathtaking. It was truly magical, but I had no idea that following that one BIG dream at the time, where I became open to who I was would bring me to this ultimate goal of creating The Intoxicator Movement. At the time, I had no friends or family around me in New Zealand, but I knew this was my dream and if I did not do it I would regret it one day.

Well I did not know it then, but at that time it was the first time I had created a space for me to become open and be who I wanted to be in the world. As I said before when I met with the recruiting company to get a job I realized it no longer matter who I was before, the only thing that mattered was how I was going to make my dream to live internationally a success, so I could be living my real-life Disney movie fairytale. My thoughts shifted immediately from looking back on my life to looking forward with my life.

I am not saying you need to move across the world to become open, but you do need to find a small way to create a consistent space to begin to follow your dream. When you do this, there will be an immediate result of self-created space for you to find your inner truth. What I mean by creating a space for yourself is that you have to actively make time to just be by yourself. This time is so important because it allows you to become open to seeing what your truth is and the possibility that you can make it a reality. Some examples of doing this is by making time in your day to sit with yourself. It can be five minutes to two hours. A few other examples of self-created space are:

- going on a walk by yourself without your phone;
- turning off your phone for a full day;
- writing down your traumatic experience or event;
- writing down positive things that happened in your day;
- going away for a weekend;
- making a habit of enjoying coffee, tea, or water with no one else around; and
- making it a habit to plan your outfit for the day instead of rushing to pick out clothes.

When I finally moved across the world, I only had me and I made a promise to myself to not fill my time with all sorts of activities like going out with friends but to take at least four hours a day for "me" time. This was an aggressive version of creating consistent space, but it led to the birth of this movement.

Once you consistently create this space, you allow yourself to become aware of all the ways your truth is trying to speak to you. You will see how you may be hiding whatever happened to you, pretending it never happened instead of embracing it. It took me about three months of giving myself four hours a day to finally learn why I had all this anger. It took me 364 hours of creating space, just me, by myself, until I finally acknowledged all the ways I had isolated myself from the world.

The way I held onto the first comment I shared with you, and connected with the boy in science class over anger, it's something I see people do every day, but they have no idea they are doing it just like not taking time to breathe deeply. I see people connecting over superficial things and comments all the time, just as I did. However, as I became open to acknowledging this comment, along with the many other small moments I connected with people, it was only because I was angry that I was given cancer. I chose not to acknowledge that cancer was only a simple word or disease that was attached to my journey; it was not the destination.

I closed myself off to the world because I thought that was the easiest way to make me feel better. I was not acknowledging that I needed to actively let go of cancer, let go of these small comments, let go of this anger because it was only allowing me to remain a victim. Subconsciously, I carried this anger around because it was in the moments of unleashing anger I felt a connection with someone, and I did not have to be vulnerable, so it felt great. It was like a consistent high I was searching for in the world because in those moments I felt alive. The problem was, it was always a negative connection, which allowed me to always suppress the truth that love will prevail. I rejected love all by myself so it never had a chance to prevail within my life. However, so many of us walk through life this way, no idea we can become open to finding our truth within.

We must acknowledge this connection with anger and hate, I keep referring to because it is something we all go through. Think of your day–to–day life. Why do you get frustrated, angry, or hold onto a grudge? This is your truth trying to speak to you and make you aware and open to seeing the unhealthy connections you may be making within your life. We each have held onto comments consciously or subconsciously in hopes of creating an instant short-term connection.

Once you become open to this, you will still experience and act in ways of anger again, but you become more self-aware of yourself, those around you, and the world. You will continue to make mistakes by saying and doing things that will hurt ourselves and others around us. The journey to becoming an Intoxicator includes acknowledging we have the power to actively become open and self-aware to the moments when we see ourselves acting in ways of hate. We become open to realizing we cannot blame the world and the people around us for an angry or stressful life. Instead we find how we can become open to our truth so we can make the world a better place.

In the becoming open step in The Intoxicator Movement, we acknowledge when the subconscious is trying to speak to us. We acknowledge our disease, and that we have the power to become open to letting go of all the anger and the injustices the world has done to us. We become open to the power we each hold. We begin to empower ourselves. The truth of becoming open is we give ourselves the key to open our heart to just be ourselves as one person in the world, no longer suppressing our truth.

When we become open, we give ourselves the opportunity to see the possibility that love can always find a way to prevail within our life and the world.

My truth when I completed this first step of becoming open to The Intoxicator Movement was acknowledging how beautiful the scar is on my neck. My scar truly looks like another smiley face. How cool is that? I have two smiles!

I challenge you in your journey through this first step to become open to the underlying gift your disease has given you.

STEP TWO

Discover

This part of our journey builds upon step one, and now we are discovering the power our truth has for us, others, and the world. Now that we are open to our truth, we allow ourselves the opportunity to discover how the truth within us guides us to our biggest, most ultimate desire, which will empower us to discover our purpose.

The world does not randomly happen to you, people do not randomly appear and disappear in your life, and your life is not filled with lucky or unlucky moments. When we begin to discover, we start recognizing the power we have within us to control the mind, body, and spirit. You hold this power over yourself, you can acknowledge this power, you can start to nurture this power, and you can actively choose to put this power toward the world. You realize you have the power to craft and create the world around you.

It took me nine years to discover I was giving away my power to cancer. I had this great energy I was freely giving away to cancer instead of putting my heart into this life, into each moment, and into my power to choose my life, to choose to create a path where love could always prevail. Instead I chose to be conquered, remain a victim of the world, and forgo my dreams, thinking there was no way they were possible.

With my disease, I subconsciously chose to discover all the ways to give my power to men, to friends, to drinking, and to drugs. But most importantly, I chose not to discover my true power and put that energy into the person I could become.

When we actively choose to begin discovering, we recognize the emotions we are holding onto from our disease. We can discover why these emotions are being generated within us, and then we can discover how to empower ourselves to become knowledgeable on how to change our negative feelings to positive. Discovering is where we empower ourselves to let our truth guide us toward our true purpose. We discover how to use our disease and put it toward what excites our heart so we can then live with our true energy, our true self and light. We can discover all the possibilities in the world for our true purpose to come alive. Above everything, we must hold ourselves accountable for discovering how to use our truth so we can become part of the momentum of moving the world forward.

In the discover step, we will begin to see we each are already imperfectly perfect. We each generate our own perfect energy, and we can overcome any disease the world gives us. We can choose to discover how we overcome it, instead of dwelling on it and letting it overtake us. We can choose any day—today, tomorrow, the next day—to start our journey to discovery.

During the discover step, we get to the place where we no longer walk through life unaware of what is going on around us. We consciously discover what is truly within us because we become open to accepting we each have this incredible power to change the world.

TIME

t is easy to get lost in time. As the world keeps spinning, time keeps on going, and sometimes it seems we end up getting lost within the world. We get so lost, so consumed, and so distracted we forget the most important things in life are the timeless moments. The moments where time does not seem to be fast or slow, it just is. Time seems to be forever in those moments. It's almost as if our heart has stopped and we forgo all of our past mistakes, all our future commitments, and we are discovering how to be completely in that moment. These are the moments we all live for, but there are healthy and unhealthy ways to discovering these timeless moments.

As humans we put ourselves in situations so we can discover feeling a certain way. We always have two choices. We can create a world where we will discover hate, anger, and loneliness, or a world where we will discover endless love, positivity, and happiness. We only live in the world we truly want to discover.

This part of discovering what was within me took years to understand. I did not even realize I was subconsciously finding a way to discover who I was in unhealthy ways. I was discovering who I was through my need for constant attention from external factors. So I never had to give myself my own attention to discover what my truth could be used for. For so long, I discovered ways to crave attention from external sources because it would always lead to me discovering all the bad in the world. Which in reality all I was doing was discovering how to manipulate myself into being a victim of the world.

Then, as I mentioned, a month after I moved to New Zealand, I discovered I could make my dream of living internationally come true on my own. Well I discovered I was still constantly reaching out to my friends from the past, wanting to FaceTime, text, catch up, and tell them all these new stories about my life instead of simply discovering this new me. This resulted in me building up more anger, frustration, and sadness because I created a need for attention from my friends to engage with my new life. Again, I fell into the trap of manipulating myself to look externally for the explanation of my own unhappiness. I discovered ways to place expectations on my friends, placing emotions on them so I did not actively have to discover how to work on myself to let go of my past.

I was across the world, choosing not to discover how to release old habits, old values, and the old me. Craving attention allowed me to find excuses on why I could not discover how to be happy on my own; instead it seemed easier to blame my friends for my own intense emotions of unhappiness. I built up so much anger and energy toward getting my attention fix that I ended a friendship with one of my good friends because he could not talk to me on his way to work. It took me about a month, but I realized I only released that anger on him because deep down, this externally strong-looking, independent, career-driven girl was lost in a dark room. When I look back now I see what a silly thing it was. Just because he could not talk or be who I needed in that moment, I chose to let my inner emotions unleash unto him. This anger wasn't about him being busy or that he couldn't talk, this anger came from me not being able to make time to discover what feelings I had within me. This built-up anger was my subconscious trying to speak to me for me to discover my own power within instead unleashing it in unhealthy ways.

Since we have become open in step one, we can now notice when our feelings of anger, sadness, or craving attention come, and acknowledge these are ways we are subconsciously hiding our root issue. Step two is actively discovering our power within these moments and choosing to discover the truth of the root issue instead of discovering the issue through superficial means.

Now that I am in the discover step, when I feel my need for attention coming on, or whatever intense negative emotion it may be, I create a space for me to discover why. I usually discover that my root issue is because I am denying myself something and I am trying to place that attention somewhere else instead of looking within. Once I become open to the truth of the root issue, I can almost instantly discover how to put that intense negative energy toward something positive. Within moments, instead of feeling angry toward a friend and wanting to lash out, I begin to give love by sharing a funny story, wishing someone a good day, or just something positive.

When I feel my intense need for attention coming on, I take time to discover what my soul is trying to say to me and discover how I can use it to positively impact the world. I no longer subconsciously walk through life discovering a world filled of hate, instead I choose to consciously discover a world full of love, a world full of people who want to use their love to make this a better place. As I have noticed, when I consciously discover a world full of love, time no longer seems to escape my life. It seems that my life becomes consumed with conscious timeless moments, the ones we all secretly crave.

THE SECOND COMMENT

This leads to the second comment I held onto. It was said by another boy in high school while I was walking down the hallway, "Oh, did your black boyfriend cut you?"

Nothing randomly happens to us, I was given cancer for a reason, to start this movement, to inspire, empower and impact people in the world to live their truth to transform the world with love. As I mentioned, we discover what we want to see in the world. I allowed this comment to lead to a whole lot of discovered anger and judgment within the world. I put responsibility on myself to try and understand how people judge others by race. Then, I added the responsibility on myself to think I had to fix the problem of unfair judgment within the world. I carried within me anger toward anyone who did judge others based on race. I would unleash anger onto my friends for making racial comments. I would put myself in situations to try and understand how someone can judge anyone based on looks.

Through this comment I discovered how to be completely consumed by what people were saying about other people, so I would only discover the bad within the world. Since I became consumed in people's judgmental reactions, I began to place judgment on others for placing judgment on others. That within itself is a hypocrisy. I by no means am saying that the comment the boy made to me is acceptable. I am saying it was not my responsibility to discover all the ways I needed to teach people that judging people because of race, looks, where they are from, or what they do is unacceptable.

All I was really achieving was noticing the problems of people, judging people, and thinking I needed to fix all of it. I discovered a world I thought needed fixing, instead of discovering a world full of opportunities to empower others. I consumed myself in only discovering the bad within the world. The whole time I held this comment subconsciously and was angry for not understanding the world or people. But in reality, I wanted to see the problems in the world so that I could blame the world for my own isolation. I continued going around the world finding ways to discover the injustices, unfairness, and awful things in the world. I chose to discover only the flaws within people who did not act in ways that showed we are all equal.

I understood the importance of discovering what we hold within us and how it can truly make the world a better place when I did a study abroad in South Africa. I went to South Africa shortly after Nelson Mandela died, and we had dinner made for us by one of the tribes. I sat with the woman who cooked us dinner, and she told me how as a young girl she saw white people kill all her family except her. I was in shock; I apologized immediately as I felt awful, but she responded saying Nelson

Mandela taught her we cannot judge based on race, gender, or where people come from, and that we must forgive and love. I remember that woman and conversation so clearly. Within a moment, this woman taught me that all over the world we are judging based on race, religion, and all sorts of things, but we must always choose to still forgive and show love to the people placing judgments who do not know any better.

In that moment, I realized I had been doing the same thing. I had subconsciously placed judgment on people who were placing judgment on others. I realized all this energy I held within I was giving away to a cause that was not moving anyone forward. It was hindering myself and the world because I was not able to create a space of love, and it was blocking myself from becoming an Intoxicator. I was doing the very thing I was angry about. Regardless of where we are from, what we look like, or what we believe, we all have the power to remove judgment. We all have the power to create space to love and forgive. We have the power to discover healthy ways to connect with ourselves and each other. When we pass judgment, we are hindering ourselves from finding common ground and creating a connection

Once you are truly within the discover step, you realize all the ways the world is trying to allow you to see love in the world. You realize the world is trying to give you the power to discover your truth. This comment said to me was that person's subconscious screaming for connection because they were very lonely and were only finding ways to reject the world around them. With this small comment, I discovered subconsciously how to let it build so much anger inside of me. It led me to so much anger over how people judge others. This anger made me feel I had to consistently be a voice to speak out against those who thought it was okay to make judgments on race. I carried this deep root of anger, not allowing myself to understand that I do not hold the responsibility of fixing this problem. The only responsibility I should hold is to discover the beauty with finding ways to show people love for being who they are, without placing judgment because that is what will start to change the world.

When we become active in discovery, we realize almost instantly when we get frustrated at others for placing judgment that we are also placing judgment. When we do this, we reject those people subconsciously, but in reality, we are rejecting ourselves because we are not creating a space of unity and potential growth toward our ultimate dream of love prevailing in this world. It is so ingrained within us to reject those who are not similar to us, those who have anything different from us, that it is easier to write these people off.

However, this is exactly what the hurtful comment did. I carried this anger and rejection for so long, even though that 16-year-old boy probably had no idea what he was saying. I could have created a space for potential growth and unity by telling him I had cancer and that guy was there for me during the surgery. But I remember I just gave him a dirty glare. I said nothing back and ran into the bathroom because I was about to start crying. I passed judgment on this person for making a racial comment and carried that anger with me, which resulted in me creating no momentum toward moving the world forward.

It only empowered me to be a hypocrite because I was passing judgment on this person for passing judgment on others.

This comment allowed me to become consciously aware of powerful emotions within, but I had no idea how to put it toward something positive. It allowed me to realize there was something inside of me to discover but that I subconsciously was putting energy toward anger because I did not know how to find healthy ways to discover we are all one. Instead when we choose to discover love to show back to a person passing judgments, eventually it will inspire them to see we should not be passing judgments onto others, especially superficial judgments.

I ask you to really look within, challenge yourself. What are comments, habits, or judgments you may be holding onto that are empowering you to discover the hate and anger within the world. What is blocking you from discovering how you can make your heart come alive again?

DISCOVER LIFE'S MEASUREMENTS

We think time is the true measurement in life, but we created time, we created the numbers we associate with time, we created that night time means it is dark, and light means it is day. However, there are moments where the world begins to seem timeless, and the world seems to stop. This is magical, right? In these moments when everything seems to align and is just perfect, it's because we have discovered consciously or subconsciously that we hold the key to discovering and creating the world within us. There is nothing but ourselves that stops us from having these timeless moments every single day of our lives. We hold the power to create a life on our own terms.

If we subconsciously feel pain within, we will discover a way to feel pain, but we will find a way to blame someone else for our pain instead of deciding to look internally to discover where that emotion is coming and why. An example of this is like my need for attention, or me holding myself responsible for fixing people who unfairly judge others. I would make myself a victim by surrounding myself with people and situations where

I allowed myself to see only the bad, but I did it because deep down, I felt bad about who I was.

A great example of the discover step is getting frustrated with coworkers. Many people have this frustration; but it's actually their subconscious trying to speak to them to have them discover the root of their frustration within themselves. Once you are open to discovery, you can shift this frustration or situation to your advantage. We become open to discovering what can we learn from these situations when frustration arises. We discover we are frustrated in another area of life and putting this onto our coworker or whoever it may be. We missed a deadline, we dropped our kids off late to school, we do not like our job—there are so many reasons for small frustrations. Instead of learning from these events in life, we might choose to put the emotional frustration onto a coworker when they could be trying to be friendly or give positive energy to us.

However, if we feel constantly certain people around us leave us with discovering negativity within, we need to discover why we are giving them power to discover this negativity within. However, there are some people who will never give us a warm, fuzzy feeling, but we have to be around them sometimes so we can figure out ways to make conversations shorter. An example is if someone asks how we are, we do not have to return the question back, this is a way to stop the conversation. This gives us the power back to go on with our day without inviting their energy into our world. When we are consciously discovering how to frame conversations, so our love and happiness within, does not get robbed by the world. When we discover how to do this we empower ourselves to grow our love to inspire, empower, and impact ourselves and others to live with truth, to guide us on the path of growing our peaceful army of love.

We usually spend so much time discovering ways to look at the external. Once we are actively open to discovering what is within, we realize we can control our world and make it full of endless positivity and love. We hold amazing power within to control our feelings, our emotions, and the world in which we live. We can learn to become actively responsible for our feelings, discover why we actually feel them, and turn that emotion into a positive experience leading us to discover who we can be within the world.

Discovering our own power seems so simple, right? But we each have subconsciously been guilty of discovering all these ways to give our power away to people, things, and the world. If you do not take time to consciously discover these consistent emotions you are feeling, you are giving your internal power away.

I think back to my life being drunk in a bar, looking for my fix at the bottom of a bottle, for any friend or guy who would talk to me; those moments are when I was screaming for love, my heart was screaming for me to love myself. However, I could not discover that because I was so busy looking for what was wrong in the world so I could blame people and the world for why I could never find love. When we start this process of looking within, it does take time, we need to be patient with ourselves, we cannot just think, "Oh, I will be open to discovery today, and everything will come and then I can be closed off tomorrow."

You need to be consciously open to discovery every day with your heart, your mind, your body.

Take one step at a time, start today with thinking about the clothes you own and wear. Do you own clothes you truly love? Do they empower you to discover how you want to present yourself, or do you own and wear clothes so you can be discovered as an image of who you think the world wants you to be?

YOUR PEOPLE

I am discussing discovery thoroughly because it is a deep, layered thought pattern. Once you are able to acknowledge each of us has undiscovered amazing power within us, your mindset will shift.

I, for so long, could not understand why some kids had to die, why some people never got to love or laugh, why families were being torn apart over money with healthcare treatments, or why some people never got to be themselves in life and had to pass away before discovering the possibility to live their truth before it was too late. I began living my day-to-day life afraid I would end up living the same experiences I witnessed these people feel: regret, anger, and hopelessness. I was afraid of ending up with no money, love, or true life when my final day came. In the American healthcare system, I saw eye-opening, shocking realities that money does tear families apart and I saw money break love. This resulted in me rejecting my truth and putting my dreams and visions to the side. I was afraid to discover if there was another path instead of the "norm" because if I followed my vision, which was just an idea, what would happen if it did not bring me money? What if the cancer came back? Would I end up in a situation with no money, ultimately be hopeless and unable to pay for a treatment that might bring me back to health. I was seeing all these injustices right before my eyes.

I subconsciously discovered how to get so addicted to unhealthy behaviors because it allowed me to feel deep, intense emotions and place blame on the world. I subconsciously choose to place responsibility on myself to try and understand the world's injustices and explore these feelings through "normal" outlets like dating, drinking, coworkers, doing jobs I hated, and the list goes on. However, it was not until much later that I realized these people, these moments, and these instances only happened to me so I could discover what was truly within me.

It was hard for me to face the truth of the discovered realities of various injustices in the world. But it felt easy for me to discover complaining and being sad about men, money, my friends, clothing, how I looked, and so on. Those things are easy for most people to relate to because its comfortable to talk about. In those discover moments, on a surface level, we are hiding our souls because we are only discovering an external, surface-level outlet to gain an instant connection to numb and suppress our soul's truth.

Once your mindset shifts, and you start consciously discovering the power you have to connect with others over your truth, you will become a magnet, attracting amazing people who are on the same journey as you. When you find these people, you often feel weird talking about things that are going on in your life at the surface level because these people are walking through life completely with their truth and are so happy doing it. When you say something outside of your truth or try to connect over a surface-level topic, they do not react, they do not give in to letting you give them your power; they simply change the subject or do not engage. These people begin to let you hold yourself to a higher standard of only communicating your truth.

You will begin to discover how to become empowered from within and then use the external world to accelerate this empowered momentum you have. You discover how to be surrounded by the people you always dreamed of being around. These are the people who feed your energy in the right direction. You will start to discover these people are already around you in so many small ways, but you never noticed it before because you were so busy discovering surface-level problems in the world. When you start to discover how to take your power back, you will see the shift within yourself.

When you are immersed in discovery, those magical timeless moments begin to occur frequently. Rush hour no longer exists because you have discovered how to make this time your time. Time for yourself, to daydream, to just be. You can choose every day what you do with this discovered truth.

The shift to discovery is in many small changes: put an inspirational sticky note in your car, play an empowering song every morning, or wear your favorite outfit to big meetings. You will start to see the shift slowly. You'll realize how people react and create space for you to discover, which results in you creating consistent space for other people to start discovering their truth.

You will realize we all are guilty and will continue to be guilty of discovering how to blame the external world; it's part of being human. However, when we commit to consciously discovering, slowly, without realizing it, we create an army of love around us, so when we start to slip back into surface-level connections, this amazing peaceful army we have crafted around us quickly brings us back to our discovered truth.

When we use unhealthy behaviors to try and discover what is within us, life keeps on spinning with no meaning. Our soul is screaming for us to begin living every day with what is within us. We owe it to ourselves to discover who we are and to the world to discover how we can live with love every day so we start to fight back against the world and create more momentum behind the truth of love.

HONESTY

Are we being honest about our discovered behaviors, habits, and thoughts? We want to be happy, and yet we often feel the world will not let us be happy.

We put our mind and body through obstacles, mindsets, and manipulations because we want to manipulate ourselves into thinking there is NO possible way we can be happy. We think everyone else just got lucky and it's not for us. I subconsciously discovered all the ways to lie and manipulate myself into thinking there was no possible way I could be happy. I subconsciously discovered how to manipulate myself to surround myself with people where the relationships would always end negatively with tons of drama. However, I subconsciously went into each of these friendships or relationships so I could discover my anger through an external factor instead of through myself. Think about this in your life, are there people or things you do around you that evoke the same negative emotions? Secretly, it's because you want to discover those things to blame the world for making it seem like there is no way your true dream or vision can come alive.

We can choose to continue manipulating ourselves as we walk through life discovering all the distractions in the world expecting external things, jobs or people to be responsible for our happiness and anger or we can discover how to align ourselves with our truth.

Once you give yourself the chance to discover why you are doing what you do day to day, you have succeeded at starting your journey to discovering what is within. Give yourself the space to think about your life and what you are giving to the world. We have such power within us that can manifest into the world, even if it's just within your family, within your house, within the city you live, or within the community you are a part of. Once you discover that this energy of yours can make the world a better place, you'll begin to live with a different flow.

As we go through this step and the process of becoming an Intoxicator, it's not that we won't ever discover frustration, sadness, or place blame, but we'll become open and aware enough to discover why we are feeling these things. At times I still carry around unworthiness within me, but I actively know it's there and know how I can discover it to then overcome it with love.

This sense of discovered worth and how we value ourselves is something we tend to deeply mask as we are swept away with the busyness of life. We get caught up in so many distractions so that we do not have to focus on what truly matters to ourselves. Instead we discover how to seek the approval of the external world and to fit into this mold that has been created.

It took me all these years and experiences to discover the light. I found so many ways to be dishonest with myself and to discover unhappiness, loneliness, and rejection in the world from buying endless clothes, drinking, dating all these guys, being addicted to social media, and the list goes on. So, I get it, I had so many awful experiences where I was sobbing because I could not understand why this was all happening to me! The truth is I subconsciously discovered how to manipulate myself into believing that the world would not let me be happy. There are SO many of us not being honest with ourselves and discovering ways to place blame on why we cannot be happy. It took me quitting my job and moving across the world just to discover I could live my dream by myself. Living my dream brought so many more amazing discoveries along the way.

Be honest with how you are discovering and what you are discovering within the world. Once you discover what your dream is, discover small ways to work toward that dream. You are then discovering how to be honest with yourself, and the world will start working in your favor because you are living your truth.

PURPOSE

The last part of discovering is how to generate excitement and self-fulfillment. We have discovered in this step the power we have within, but now we discover how we will let ourselves be excited.

When I started this book about my cancer saga, it was a way to start this communication with you. While it was my life, it was really a way to discover how to use my story for us to relate, because as I said the birth of our connection, what we all have in common is relating we can to overcoming a struggle. Almost everyone has been affected in some way by cancer or their own disease. This whole story of cancer, men, and friends is so we can relate to each other and then have the opportunity to acknowledge we do have the choice to discover what is within us. We have suffered from similar issues or different issues, but we have discovered the same emotional feelings. We suffer the same heartaches, and we feel the same excitement and love, just through different stories, different events that have happened to us. It is nothing more than a story within our lives that evokes the same emotions between us.

When we connect over our power within, we generate passion in our lives. Passion is what needs to be created in order for us to move onto the next step. Step two, includes the discovery of who we are, discovering how to create passion around our truth, and then discovering how to put this energy into the world. When we share our discovery of who we are with the world, we start to create empowerment for ourselves and those around us. When we authentically live with who we are, this allows other people to discover who they are because they see happiness come out of us by simply being ourselves. They are able to see that through your new day-to-day life, magic is happening for you. Slowly the people around you want to reach within to discover what they have within.

Imagine a world where people start to ask you about your passion in depth. Imagine you start unleashing your true purpose, excitement, and love back into the world. Every day you feel yourself giving this love and excitement. Imagine how your body, mind, and soul would respond and react to life?

This whole book, my stories, and lessons I have gone through are simply showing that I had the power to discover who I was within and to change who I was pretending to be. I chose for nine years to live a life full of fun on the outside, but it was always dark on the inside. It took me moving to New Zealand to isolate myself from the world to discover I wanted to impress myself. That all this success would keep coming, but I would still feel empty because I was living this life not for myself but to fit a mold. I struggle at times to fight the urge to fit a mold when I tell people about The Intoxicator Movement. However, I am always able to overcome these feelings because I know now that I have discovered my purpose to intoxicate the world with love and to empower people to courageously live their truth to make this world a better home for all of us.

When I truly had the courage to complete the discover step of the movement was when I hired my business coach to start this movement. I finally allowed myself to discover that there was a possibility I could live with my true purpose in the world every day.

STEP THREE

Explore

This is the MOST exciting step of the Intoxicator journey. In this step, you are out in the world, putting language to your movement, finding ways to explore yourself in healthy lifestyle choices.

This is the part where we give ourselves permission to start exploring all the ways we can begin creating our truest, most powerful dream lifestyle. We have become open to acknowledging that we have the choice to create our life by choosing to discover what we see within ourselves, people, and the world. Step three, explore, is where we will learn how to actively put ourselves around people, engage in activities, and create a lifestyle that empowers us to always explore our truest self within the world. The exploring step is where we hold ourselves accountable to only engage in activities that empower us to explore what we have discovered is within us.

To open the explore step, we will go through this story: We have decided to go to a concert with a friend, but at the last minute this friend says they can no longer attend.

Before starting our journey on becoming an Intoxicator most of us would reply with,

"That is so irresponsible. I am so angry, and I am so sad our friend always does this."

However, on our journey we have become open to acknowledging those feelings are our subconscious trying to speak to us. As we went through step two, discovery, we discovered we create our world around us.

In the explore step, we hold ourselves accountable for acknowledging we only in engage in activities that let us explore our truth. We go to a concert regardless of whether or not a friend comes with us, because we want to attend this concert to explore our truth through music at a venue with hundreds or thousands of other people who also enjoy the music we do. Being able to experience the concert with your friend would have been a bonus, but no matter what you can be happy to explore yourself by engaging in this activity alone or with someone. When we are truly immersed with the exploring step, we begin to hold ourselves responsible that we would only be going to the concert or event because that is what we truly wanted to do.

This step is learning how to actively engage ourselves with people and activities that align with what we have discovered truly excites us and lets us explore who we are. We hold ourselves responsible for acknowledging when we have put ourselves in a position to do something that does not excite us, that we are not exploring who we truly are within the world.

I am not saying we do not ever have to compromise for those we love: children or family.

I'm saying you have already discovered you are the one who has the power to control your life. If someone asked you to go to a concert and you said, "Yes, I want to go to the concert," that is because you sincerely know this is something you would have done alone or with a friend, because it's a vehicle that lets you explore your truth.

Let's bring this back to your everyday habits. Think of all the opportunities you have to explore yourself. Take a moment to write down the last time you let yourself be filled with love and happiness because you did something you really enjoyed.

Again, if you are at this step and still have the mindset of thinking this is stupid, please go back and reread the first and second step. By writing down in this book your most recent experience of love and happiness, someday someone will pick up this book and get to read about someone else's day filled with joy.

_____

_____

_____

_____

_____

_____

The reason I had you write this down is so I can challenge you. I am positive the time you wrote about was a time when you were exploring you in your truest and happiest self. This step is about learning how to capitalize on all the opportunities in your life through your kids, your job, your health, your partner, your friends, and so on, to be your truest and happiest self. This step is all about acting on opportunities to put yourself around people, situations, and events that empower you to explore what is within you.

In this step, I started with the example of the concert so you can see a small way we can change behaviors, patterns, and actions to explore healthy ways to create your dream lifestyle. I will go deeper in this step and explain how I explored my inner passions in unhealthy ways. I ask you to please meet me halfway as you read this book, pour your heart out, and open your mind to get a glimpse at finding ways to explore what you have discovered within. This will enable you to start unleashing the true inner love, beauty, innovation, and success of a life you deserve to live. We each hold the responsibility to ourselves to engage in activities that let us explore who we truly are. We each have the power to change how we explore ourselves in the world so we can be empowered to unleash our inner love, innovation, beauty, and success to live our dream lifestyle.

THE THIRD COMMENT

The third comment I mentioned in the beginning of the book happened when a guy at a party came up and asked me, "Did some guy choke you out during sex?"

This comment was the aggressive birth of exploring the anger and loneliness I felt because of cancer through other people. This comment escalated my extreme, intensive dating hobby that I used to place blame on the world.

Through my dating hobby, I subconsciously found ways to explore my problems through men. I would date all these guys, and text men at all hours of the day and night, just so I could create an ending to each relationship that would allow me to explore placing blame for a broken heart, hurt feelings, feeling used, feeling angry, feeling sad, and most importantly feeling unworthy. However, I could blame all these "feelings" on some-one else instead of having to look within to explore my truth. I could go through each of the numerous guys and tell the sob story of what happened, but the reality is each story does not matter because it was just a way for me to explore the emptiness I felt within and place external blame.

I created this hobby of obsessing over guys. I would wonder what they thought of my text. I would craft how I should talk on the phone or in a text. I would get wasted so that I would have to be taken care of, and I would only wear clothes that brought me attention based on my body's features. I walked a certain way to get noticed, I posted pictures only to get attention, and I only talked to my girlfriends about guys. I thought most girls were just as obsessed with this dating hobby as I was. I didn't realize that with other girls I could have explored sports, reading, laughter, movies, art, getting our nails done, or talking about real issues within the health system or cancer. I created this whole hobby to use men as an outlet to subconsciously explore my own anger, unworthiness, insecurities, and unhappiness, and then place blame on the world for why I could not be myself.

Eventually this hobby of using men to explore how I was feeling began to not be enough. The feeling of unworthiness resurfaced more and more quickly, so I found another way to try and explore myself in the world by creating a friend hobby. My friend hobby was very similar to my dating hobby. I wanted to be friends with anyone and everyone. I would meet people and put all this effort into them. Immediately after I met them, I would say, "We're best friends." I poured myself into a new friend all day, every day. We would text, go swimming, talk about what to wear, get drunk, and most importantly we could talk about our guy drama. It was perfect for me to have new friends to talk about guys with, so it never became too repetitive for any one friend. I could always bring the conversation back to men and feed my addiction of using men as a vehicle of communication to unleash my true anger, unworthiness, and suppressed feelings that came with my cancer.

I was watching a documentary on Gaia, *Healing the Luminous Body: The Way of the Shaman,* by Dr. Alberto Villoldo and he mentioned a woman he worked with and how she came to realize she had dated seven different guys, but the relationships all ended the same. She was not learning the lesson and kept dating the same type of guy. Within that moment, I realized the truth. I was holding onto this comment and creating my dating and friend hobby so I could explore my anger with cancer, my insecurities with how I looked, and creating rejection of myself through guys and friends, so I could blame the world for my pain. Within that moment, I released exploring myself through other people because I realized I had the power to explore my dream lifestyle myself.

Take the time to think of a comment or situation that has hurt you, that you may carry with you, and acknowledge your "dating hobby or friend hobby." (Your hobby may be the same or may be different, but take time to look within and acknowledge it.) Begin to see the possibility that you could explore that problem within yourself instead of through other people. What if you gave yourself the gift to acknowledge this and actively found ways to explore your true self within the world?

I have crafted this vision of a world of Intoxicators so you can finally explore you. You won't feel the need to explore yourself in unhealthy ways; instead explore your truth because it will make you feel more alive in the world than you have ever felt before.

CHOICES

created my dating and friend hobbies to explore the guilt I felt for beating cancer. I felt guilty that there were kids dying; I felt guilty when I saw marriages being torn apart because parents could not save their kids' lives due to financial reasons; and I felt unworthy to be living because it was not fair. All of this guilt and anger started to build up when I was 14 and it continued, but I explored these emotions through my men and friend hobby.

I used all these discovered feelings to explore scenarios where I could not be who I wanted to be in the world. Holding onto these negative comments allowed me to explore only liking guys that I thought needed fixing. I was exploring who I was through these various guys, placing expectations on them to give me affirmation that I was achieving success. However, this was set up for failure because I was creating a lifestyle for myself where I would always need someone else to affirm for me I was going on the right path, instead of the affirmation coming from within.

I was trying to explore who I was in the world by going to parties and putting myself in situations where people thought these types of comments were okay to say. I put myself around people who were not ready to be open to discovering and exploring who they were. I was exploring what I wanted to accomplish in the world through men so I could reach the same conclusion that it was impossible to transform a powerful vision into reality. I was allowing myself to feel this way because that is what I thought I deserved.

We only choose to explore who we are in the world to get a given outcome. I created a dating and friend hobby because I wanted to explore being rejected, angry, lonely, and sad through other people so I did not have to make myself accountable to choose to become better. I thought the world did not give me a choice to be vulnerable and explore my truth. As soon as I watched, *Healing the Luminous Body*, I saw the possibility that I actually had the choice to explore my truth in the world. Once I decided to hold myself accountable and chose to demand my dreams into reality, I became unstoppable because I no longer explored myself in environments, people, and hobbies that were not my truth.

We always have the choice to find a way to explore ourselves in healthy lifestyle choices and to give ourselves the power to no longer remain a victim of the world we have created. Reflect on your life, think for a moment, when do those timeless moments seem to appear in your life, the ones you wish you could have all the time. Whatever those moments are, start putting your energy toward making those moments happen more frequently.

MOMENTUM

We only see what we want to see in the world. We do not all have a dating hobby, but we all have an unhealthy hobby we've engaged in. This can vary from drinking, drugs, going out, dating, overeating or undereating, being a workaholic. We become addicted to something so we can explore our problems through that vehicle. This goes back to becoming open to my root issue of overcoming cancer, coming to terms with what that meant, and how I wanted that experience to shape me going forward.

I let this small comment, "Did a guy try to choke you out during sex," become the controlling factor of my life. We all have comments that are said to us that are mean and unfair and things we do not deserve to hear. However, these comments only have as much meaning as we let them have. I only created my dating hobby to get my fix for connection, to get my fix of being understood in the world. I did not hold myself responsible for knowing how to be open about these issues and discovering the root. Life will consist of moments and comments said to us, like this comment said to me. We can either let these comments negatively impact us and find unhealthy ways to explore ourselves, or we can explore who we truly are and, in the process, make the world a better place.

The first time I saw a glimpse of hope to let myself be free and explore who I was in a healthy way with someone was my sophomore year of college. I finally let myself have a friendship. For the first time I did not explore my life filled with judgments, trying to fix him, trying to explore my life through him. I would go over and find food at his house because I wanted to hang out, he would come over and watch movies, he'd have all my girlfriends over for drinks before going out. It was the first friend I shared my journey with him instead of exploring all my problems through someone.

I remember I was having one of my mental breakdowns because of some guy that I thought broke my heart, when I really broke my own heart. He would always somehow pull me back to life, to not just talk about the guy but to also talk about dancing, food, silliness. He let me be free the way I truly want to be free. (These are the type of people you attract in your life in the discover step, when you discovered the possibility of living your truth.) He really was the person I allowed to empower me to discover that I can explore myself in the world and that it will be enough. He was the one who always believed in my vision and empowered me to explore it and live it.

It is a good feeling when you wake up and you are exploring yourself in healthy choices in life to make your dreams come true. You will no longer need to have a reason why you are doing the things you do because you're exploring the rhythm within you and putting language to your movement. When you start to do this, movement occurs fluidly because you realize the power within and everything you are doing is for something bigger than yourself. This is when you really get to the depth of exploring and see yourself as part of the bigger picture. You do not have to describe everything you are doing because you are doing it for the bigger picture and purpose of your life. This is when time starts to fly. The exploration step is when momentum begins to build in your life, for you to reach your ultimate goal to live your fairytale dream, a life with no regrets.

GO OUT AND EXPLORE

This is your shot!

This is the part of the book where you are now completely aware of the subconscious habits and behaviors in your life. This is the part where you realize you can do this: you can take back your responsibility, take back your love, take back what you are giving to other people, and explore you! Explore things that will put you outside your comfort zone; push yourself to your limits so you can truly grow.

An example: I am not a yoga professional, but I enjoy it to clear my mind and heal my body. I went to a handstand vinyasa class. I could not do a handstand and was a bit nervous about going, but I figured, let's try something new, explore a handstand. This class was the coolest thing because I got to acknowledge this power I had within me! I got to explore my mind and self while trying to use all my strength to lift my body into the air to fly. This is one small example where I found a way to explore myself.

When you are truly exploring, you begin to acknowledge the skills and powers other people have, and you surrender yourself to not having to know everything! You surrender yourself to explore your own truth. You no longer need to be the best at everything; just start exploring your truth in this world around us! Act on what you have discovered your truth to be and explore; let your truth shine through.

Once I started to let myself explore, that is when it all came together. I took one step at a time. I slowly realized I didn't need to be afraid of being alone again. If I was exploring my truth, everything else would fall into place. But we all do this; we are in fear that if we explore what excites us, we may be rejected by our current friends, work, or lifestyle. We get so caught up in this fear of rejection, of being alone, we never start to explore. We go back to manipulating ourselves subconsciously to live a life not true to us. Which as we know, builds up anger, even more loneliness, and rejection.

Instead, go explore the world, explore what excites you, and know that someone out there has that same passion! Go live. It does not need to be a huge, earth-shattering step. Start by wearing your favorite color, joining an athletic team once a month, or cleaning your room so it feels nice and fresh. Go for a walk on your lunch break, or leave work early to go jam out in your car. If you start to explore and people reject you, courageously and unapologetically say goodbye. People or hobbies that reject you for your actual truth only liked you for the illusion you were showing the world. You cannot attract the greater things into your life that represent your truth until you let go of living a lie.

Let go of the mask. The people who reject you without the mask are rejecting themselves because they are seeing the courage you have to live your truth, and they cannot find that same courage within. When you think about it, how can we reject anyone for trying to live their truth?

Today is your day! No need to let the subconscious control your life a moment longer. There will always be moments of discomfort, but the discomfort will only get worse if you keep surrendering your life to your untrue self! Take back the power you are giving away, tune into your subconscious, and begin to explore yourself. I promise if you try one small thing to explore your truth, your fairytale dream will start to come true.

We wake up every day with the opportunity for our day to be filled with surprises, plans, and unfilled moments waiting to be filled. Choose to live each day to the fullest. We do have some obligations usually, but even so, our day is made up of moments that arise. You will notice within yourself when you start to be actively engaged with the explore step, you will become one with who you are. You are no longer hiding or pretending to be someone you were taught to be. Magic will start to appear in your life, the same way my first real friend appeared in my life.

In the beginning of step three, I asked you to write about a time you were filled with love and happiness. Imagine if you made it part of your lifestyle to explore yourself every day. Can you imagine what a world it would be if we all held ourselves accountable for creating infinite life moments filled with our truth—moments filled with exploring our truth through love, happiness, sadness, and anger, too? Imagine a world full of exploring people, where we all impact the world with our truth.

My truth of when I completed the explore step was when I spent $5,750 NZD, to go to an entrepreneur retreat in Fiji with 200 other entrepreneurs, specifically from New Zealand. Many of these entrepreneurs are globally or nationally recognized. Here I was, a 24-year-old American girl, with an idea, no actual business yet, spending WAY above my budget to go explore my purpose. I was there to explore to find a way to make my dream work. I was immersed in the explore step because I was doing everything my soul loved: immersing myself within my purpose and passion, traveling, and empowering myself to be surrounded by tons of other successful people impacting the world. It gave me courage to see that love will always win. This was the truth of me exploring my ultimate self. It was what scared me and excited me, but that is how I knew I was ready to move onto the next step. I hope you explore your power within to inspire yourself, to explore new limits, not only so your aware of your ultimate truth but that you are able to start living it.

STEP FOUR

LOVE

T his step is the most empowering because it walks us through loving who we are every day as we grow and evolve. We have already created a life where we are actively engaging in activities that allow us to explore who we truly are within the world. We will now go through how to acknowledge our darker side, use that as motivation to fuel our "why," and we will learn how to always embrace our brightest moments!

When loving ourselves, we should not shy away from our dark side. The darkness within us is what can be used to motivate us to use our gifts and change the world. We learn that we will not *always* be happy and living a life full of joy, but we learn to love the moments of sadness, despair, anxiety, anger, and so on, because we can actively choose to explore these times with healthy lifestyle choices so we can create higher impact in the world.

On this part of the journey, we learn to accept and love every single part of us because that is what make us, us. There is no one else in the world exactly like you. We journey through learning to love every part of ourselves—the good and the bad. This seems like such an easy concept, loving ourselves. But on this journey, we have learned that subconsciously we seek love from external factors. This step is about truly making sure we are taking time to discover long-lasting fulfilling love from within. We want to treat ourselves with so much love and care that we set the correct boundaries and always feel at home within. When we nurture this home from within, we allow ourselves to become safe from rejection because we no longer reject ourselves. These boundaries empower us to accept only treatment we deserve. We create a life filled with meaningful moments shared with people we love. If we do not love ourselves, the best moments with others cannot truly be lived because we were not being who we truly are. Once we actively decide to be authentically who we are in the world, instead of fighting it, it will guide us to find our internal home.

THE FOURTH COMMENT

The final comment I held onto in order to remain a victim of my story is very intense. But it's crucial to understanding how deeply the subconscious can mask the screams for connection.

A boy I didn't even know, asked me at a frat party, "Are you okay? Did you try to kill yourself?"

I held onto this comment; I allowed it to be my excuse for why I was insecure about who I was and how I looked. The last thing I wanted was people actively asking me if I tried to kill myself because I had a scar on my neck from cancer. I used this comment to consistently place blame on why I could not just feel like a normal teenager. I held onto this comment as a reason for why I could not go out of the house, as a reason that I deserved to have no friends, and as a way to place blame on the world around me for being so awful.

I remember this comment so clearly because it took everything inside of me to not break down right in that moment, to just release the sadness that I allowed to come over me. This comment was truly a way I was able to release my sadness and anger with cancer. I am not making excuses for the guy who made this comment, but this comment was external to me. I could not control what people said to me, I could only control how I reacted.

Let's review this comment through step one to this step, step four. In step one, we became open to realizing these comments are not about us. The comments people say to us, about us, or about others are cries for connection. That guy saw my neck and that sparked his subconscious to speak that question. This was his form of trying to connect with someone who may be in this dark space with him. Then moving into the step two, discover, we learned we can only discover things within other people that we discover in ourselves. This young man, whom I barely remember, must have spoken these words to me because he was going through depression or wanting to kill himself. This is not a question a happy, fulfilled person would ask a random stranger. This comment was his subconscious giving a cry for connection. This young man was hurting and he saw a moment to try to connect, so he asked this question. In step three, explore, I was exploring myself in unhealthy environments to evoke these comments around me, so I could place blame on others and the world for being so awful.

At age 19, when this comment occurred, I did not have enough wisdom or knowledge to know this was a cry for connection. Instead I used this comment to be a victim. In reality, he was 1 person out of 300 people at the party. That's less than 1% of the people at the party. After this comment, I made it impossible to give anyone a chance to get close to me. I never opened myself up so I could avoid any portion of sadness that I allowed from this comment. I isolated myself from the good and the bad of the world. In step four, we learn to love ourselves, and that's what can make us immune to comments like this.

At the time, I allowed this comment to kill me inside. I used this comment to find all the things wrong with me, all the reasons why I should not just accept how I looked or who I was and to not go into the world with an open heart. In reality if I would have replied with a simple, "No, my scar is from cancer," I would have showed vulnerability (which at the time seemed impossible). However, I looked at him with a blank face, walked away, got in a cab, and sobbed the whole way home. If I would have shared the truth, it would have created a safe place, allowing him to share something vulnerable back with me. I could have created a loving space where we connected positively. Instead I put myself in a completely isolated room. I cried and cried, wishing that I was pretty, wishing that I was invisible.

In this step, love, we walk through this comment and the comments that have been said to you, and we learn to choose to love ourselves, to love our story. We can see that we have the power to choose to look at other people and the world from a perspective of love. These comments can be thrown at us in intense ways, but we will always come back to center to experience the love we have created within. Through this journey, we have built a safe home within and will continue to infinitely grow our love within that home. We learn to love the truth of who we are.

BE THE LOVE

In the love step, we realize the comment, "Are you okay? Did you try to kill yourself?" is a deep call for connection. Think about this for a moment. Would you randomly ask a stranger you just met that question?

No.

The only reason someone would think to say something like that is because they're exploring what is on their mind, and they don't know how to do it in a healthy way.

In this step, we truly begin to see the depths the subconscious goes to in order to mask the scream for love and connection, from ourselves, others, and the world. In step four, love, we now realize when others speak to us in harsh ways, it is actually their subconscious screaming for love. They are carrying around unworthiness but have not consciously come to terms with it, so their subconscious is begging to connect with someone, but unfortunately it comes out through an unhealthy avenue. When we begin to be immersed in the love step, we understand this and can act back in a loving way to these people. I am not saying we will become best friends with them or that it is our duty to be the connection they crave.

Regardless of a comment, behavior, habit, or situation that happens to us, we can choose to love. We can choose to not let this comment disrupt our loving home within. We have the knowledge to accept we all make mistakes; we all have craved love in an unhealthy way. When these comments do happen in front of you, you owe this person, and the world, to be the light in that moment by giving back in a way of love. Even the smallest act of love has a huge effect.

Regardless of the degree of truth to a comment or rumor said about us, when we respond with love, we are showing people that the world is not all bad. When we give this small token of kindness back to this person, this one small kind act will undo ripples of anger and hurt they carry within. You might never see this person again, you might never get to see how this small comment impacted this person for the better, but you will know that you acted in a way of love to impact someone who was in a dark room. You created an act of kindness, an act of love for someone because you have worked on creating home from within. Now you know these comments and rumors can no longer get to you. You love yourself, you realize the amazing power you hold within you, and you are beginning to see how the love you hold within can become a resource to the world around you.

LIGHT WITHIN DARKNESS

You will go about life actively choosing to be the love in every situation, but unworthiness will resurface from time to time. On this journey, you have found all the new ways to be you and how to constantly find new ways to explore you. You begin to realize the world needs you—not you pretending to be someone else. This should inspire you to love yourself and create a home within.

It is important to touch on the darkness of what is within us as well though. During the time I was writing this book, while I was experiencing the love step, I felt darkness come over me in an extremely intense way.

I felt paralyzed. I felt empty. I felt depressed., My heart dropped. I could not quite grasp it; it felt like I wanted to vomit in the middle of my stomach. I felt dark energy within that was trying to release itself, but I just could not figure out what it was. I felt this dark energy trying to control my mind. I felt myself wanting to give up all this love stuff because I was not sure it was actually true.

I caught up with a friend, and I allowed myself to be put in a place where I was explaining my new life. I was craving recognition and affirmation that I was on the "right" path. The darkness poured over me, and I knew this was part of the journey. I was exploring my dreams through this friend, talking about visions, plans, and what I was doing to work toward creating The Intoxicator Movement to intoxicate the world with love. I realized I was only going on about my plans and ideas so I could receive recognition from an external source. And, guess what? This friend mostly rejected my ideas.

At that exact moment, when the darkness came over me, I realized I was giving my power of love for myself away because I wanted recognition from the world for being who I truly was. I didn't know where the darkness was coming from inside me, but I knew my need to control the unknown, my need to be loved, and that my need to feel secure in that moment was intense. When these issues arose from within, I acknowledged I was exploring myself in an unhealthy way. I then chose to accept and love myself for these feelings because it is part of who I am.

I allowed myself to be put in a place where I felt insecure, I allowed myself to question my whole being and all this work I had done. I again put myself in a place to tell myself I was stupid, unworthy, and that there was no way love could always win. In reality I wanted to throw myself this little pity party because I could not give up my need for control, my desire to know that I was on the right path. I wanted to cry. I wanted to break down. I wanted to scream and yell; honestly, I wanted to release this darkness because I was so sick of thinking and hearing that love could not always win

In this moment, I chose to look at myself with love. I knew my mission was bigger than myself. I knew that I had given love and spread it into the world, but I still could not fully do it for myself. I look back at this situation now and see I hoped to get affirmation that I was on the right path, but that would have been a temporary fix of love—not fulfilling, long-lasting love. In step four, you are able to look at these moments as motivation. Now I find the strength to explore this intense, dark energy within, to then love even deeper what I hold within, no matter what darkness overcomes me.

I am human, so my soul still screams at me to stop allowing myself to get to this space. I still sometimes have negative self-talk, but I realize this immediately and decide to love myself and understand it's part of the human process to reach my ultimate, greatest self-love. The root of not being able to accept your inner darkness is fear—fear that you may reject yourself or the world may reject you for this darkness. But in reality, we all have darkness, and this is part of the process for every single one of us. The love step is learning how to find the light within our darkness to create the greatest self-love.

I want this next point to really sink in, so truly dig deep and apply it to your life. Within love, we start to acknowledge, accept, and understand that we each hold darkness within. We cannot fight against it with resistance, but we have created a peaceful army of love together. So, when the darkness comes over us, we have a tribe around us conquering that darkness with love.

TUNE INTO YOUR PASSIONS

tep four empowers us to know that our passions will not include everything in the world. We do not need to be knowledgeable about every topic or be the best at everything. When we accept that we do not need to be passionate about everything in the world, the world will give us the people, resources, and tools to surround us where our passions do not lie. When we release the need for control, of having to be the best, we will find there are so many moments that arise where people show up wanting to empower you with their passion in life. After a while, it becomes liberating. Now you can focus on what generates energy within your soul, and the world gives you other people to complement you while they live their soul's truth.

Here's a small example: I love working out, but I am not the scientific, body person, the structured workout teacher, or anything in that realm. Instead of pretending I am that person or trying to spend time figuring out how to be that person, I always find a workout place every time I move. I decide to not spend my time teaching myself full-blown workout classes because that is not where my passion lies. Instead of spending time and energy on something that does not light me up inside, I make time to find the right experts to empower me reach new goals with my personal fitness. Since I do this, I do not have to worry about figuring out how to push my body every day. I show up to a yoga studio, gym, or personal fitness class, and all that time and energy I was using before to figure out my fitness game is now free again to focus on my true passion.

The lesson here is that when we can accept we are not passionate about everything, we allow ourselves to release the need for control at having to be the best at everything. We can seek out others that will empower us to reach our goals. We reach a new level of love from within. When we go to personal trainers, business strategists, or Intoxicator strategists, we are allowing ourselves to become empowered. We allow experts filled with passion in their field to create plans for us. This empowers us to become even better at our passion because we free up time and energy within our mind to focus on what truly matters to our soul. We do not have to do all of life alone; we have each other for a reason. We have the power to create connections, be vulnerable, and become empowered by others in positive ways. When we are vulnerable, we seek assistance, and we seek to have others empower us to reach our untapped potential. That is the beauty of connection, self-love, and giving love to others; they can use their passion to empower you to succeed. When you are honest with loving yourself, you will impact the world in bigger ways, and the world will impact you in greater and more intense ways as well.

Fully embrace who you are, absolutely love yourself, and share that love with the world to become part of the momentum to move the world forward. It is so ingrained in us to want to suppress our truth. It seems too crazy to simply love who we are and be that. But this is where we must actively let go of everything external that is not part of who we are. Let go of trying to be the expert workout guru, then let go of the wrong career path, negative thought patterns, or whatever it is that is not your truth.

REAL LOVE

Real love is imperfectly perfect. Real self-love and loved shared with those you surround yourself with will be filled with, happiness, sadness, laughter, worry, joy, and so many other things because that love is real. As I started this movement, I obsessed over the truth of my theory, worried that love may not always be the answer. I didn't realize I could love myself even when things weren't going well. I was not finding ways to love every part of me. I had to experience situations that contained darkness so I could believe in myself without relying on the world to fill me up. The intense darkness that came over me with cancer and each of the four comments had to occur so I would challenge myself to accept my true self. This story had to be shared because it shows that this movement I created will not always be butterflies; it is about learning to love every single part of us as life occurs.

We all have a disease the world has given to us that will always be part of who we are because it's the foundation of our connection with others, it allows us all to relate to the struggle we have gone through. This disease is why we thought we had to hide ourselves; it is why we have our darkness; it is why we start to become open to being vulnerable with the world. This disease is something we need to make peace with. The disease, the darkness, and the lows we need to begin to embrace and love because it is part of our journey. We cannot push ourselves to new highs, new happiness, and new love if we do not fully acknowledge the lows. This movement challenges us to strive for real love, which is filled with ups and downs. The love step is the true shift of self-awareness to accept we will still feel the need for control, for perfection, and to seek approval from the world, but we will learn to love each of these intense energies because they empower us to appreciate the highs even more intensely.

I am only writing this story and these intense feelings that resurface within me because that is real. That will happen, and instead of fighting these feelings, love them, find a place within your internal home to make it safe to have these things occur. You will have the need for power, the need for money, the need for control, the need for perfection come up—they will never go away; it's human nature. In this step, we learn to love these feelings, accept them, and know they are only coming upon you for something greater to soon come along.

Sometimes we think we need a "huge" breakthrough, something to make us better, but sometimes we just need to accept we will be filled with negativity. We will be filled with negativity in the short term because in the longer term it's pushing the intensity of our emotions to new boundaries. Loving is tough, it is imperfect, it is not always fun, but in the long run this is what allows us to live a fulfilled life. If we suppress these feelings, they will only get more intense, and we will subconsciously create a box to isolate us from the world, as I did with the fourth comment said to me. Appreciate that this is life; it is ups and downs—like a heartbeat. As you grow in love, the more intensely life happens for you, the more we need to have these healthy outlets to release this energy within. Release this power because you are the power, you are the energy, you are the light, you are the love that the world needs.

The true love in this step is knowing that you are being authentically you every day with the good and the bad, but you are empowered because you acknowledge the world needs you. The world needs you to be you, so you can change the world with your unique passions and gifts. The world needs you being you, so you are happy, and so you are living with love. The time to start loving yourself is now, not tomorrow or weeks from now, but today. There is no right or wrong way to start your story of goodbye to who you are pretending to be. The time is always there to start choosing to love yourself. You hold the power to choose your life moments and the power to start the beginning of who you truly are.

What a world it would be if we did not compete with each other for the most knowledge or to be the smartest in the room. Instead we just love who we are, we do not pretend to be something we are not, and we empower others to live a life filled with love by intoxicating them though our passions. Everyone deserves love, everyone deserves to win in life, everyone deserves to live their dreams, and everyone deserves to intoxicate the world with love. My truth of when I completed the love step was when I was fully able to embrace that I want the world to be my home. I want a world where I have universal passport, intoxicating the world with love, spreading this message to inspire, empower, and impact people to live their truth. So many people rejected this dream of mine, telling me I was absolutely crazy for it, but now I embrace my dream. I am living it and I am transforming the world with love. I would not change who I am for anything because it is what has brought us here today. I hope in this step you find your irresistible passion and love from within, regardless of how crazy or wild your dream seems to the rest of the world, learn to embrace it, and to see the power within so you can move onto the final step.

I finally let go of the mold of the world I was trying to fit into and embraced the love I had for when I started this movement and became the full-time love girl. My truest, most powerful self-love where I risked it all was when I gave my four-week notice to my corporate job in New Zealand foregoing my yearly commission check, with only $5,000 USD in savings and increased my credit limit in case of emergency to $20,000. I did this without the movement fully being relaunched, without this book being completely done with editing, but deep down I knew that it was the right moment.

I was working with my editor, my digital strategist, a copywriter for my bio, and a book cover designer. It was my moment to use my filled-up heart of love to launch The Intoxicator Movement. I was ready to inspire, empower, and impact people to live their truth without having to go through all the pain I put myself though. That was the moment I embraced all the love I had within to trust that my vision of this movement would create high impact by intoxicating every soul searching for their truth. This was my moment of truth in the love step, when I was finally living in the world with my truest self-love. I was no longer putting myself in situations to be rejected. At this point, I knew I had finally completed loving myself and could move on to the last and final step.

STEP FIVE

INTOXICATOR

At age 23, I put my theory together, my vision out in the world with the intention to intoxicate the world with love. I was hoping to create a ripple effect. I've crafted my vision into a reality because it was the first time in my life I put my whole heart, blood, sweat, and tears into something. It was the first time I let the world see my vulnerabilities, my passion, and my darkness. It was the first time I believed in myself. I know that becoming an Intoxicator is something we should all strive for because we all deserve to courageously live our truth in the world. We each hold the global world in our hands with the opportunity to become part of the momentum to make the world a better place.

An Intoxicator is someone who takes time to create space, to look within, remove the toxic, and become what is left: your truth in the world. This is the most magical place—where you live your life every day, intoxicating the world just by being you! Step five has no negative comment because this is where we are no longer a victim of any one comment. We have completely let go of any external factors, external blame, or using past stories to justify not being happy. We are now living with no regrets because we are giving our truest self to the world every day.

This step recognizes we will have tough days, but we do not let the tough days filled with darkness take over or allow them to isolate us from the rest of the world. We no longer let these dark emotions or negative things take over because we have gone through the journey and know how to acknowledge them, discover how these emotions are created within us, and then explore them in a healthy way into the world around us.

This last step is about intoxicating the world with love by finding all the ways to create space to give love into the world. In the Intoxicator step, we now see all the unhealthy ways people subconsciously manipulating themselves to get an instant-short lived connection. An Intoxicator actively sees people doing this and chooses to create moments filled with love to empower people to see a world filled with love.

Lastly, this step reviews how we hold ourselves responsible to always be true to ourselves. We realize we will always be going on the Intoxicator journey throughout our life as we grow and evolve. We learn that this journey can be applied over and over again to our lives, so we're always reaching for higher goals and increasing love within ourselves and the world.

Our connection through this book is a moment of celebration, filled with passion and excitement. You have joined the movement of becoming an Intoxicator, you have committed to going on this journey to always be the real you in the world. You'll continue on this path to reach new love within yourself, others, and the world.

THE INTOXICATOR TRUTH

A true Intoxicator is very similar to this analogy:

I am walking on a beach and there are hundreds of thousands, millions, or maybe even billions of starfish on the beach. I go there by myself to start throwing them back into the water. You see me and come along the beach beside me to throw the starfish back into the water too. As you start doing this with me, someone else walks along and starts to throw the starfish in the water. Eventually there are tons of people throwing the starfish back into the water to keep them alive. We may never get to everyone, but at least we started the momentum.

This is the story of an Intoxicator. I started this movement for people like you, people like me with very ordinary lives, trying to overcome the disease the world has given us. With people like you and me, the starfish have the possibility of not only become alive again, but they can start to live a life with this new-found sense of purpose because they were able to continue to keep on living because someone empowered them to keep on living, by taking the time to throw them back in the water. That is the same as a real-life Intoxicator, with people like you and me, being our true selves and actively giving more love into the world, we are empowering people to have a greater sense of life. As an Intoxicator, we do this day in and day out within our home, our town, our city, our state, our country, and the world. We create a space for others to feel safe to be themselves, and they can start to live with this new profound sense of purpose, because they see the possibility that they can just live their truth, without the mask and it will be enough.

This is the moment I realized I was a true Intoxicator:

I had gone to have drinks with two of my friends who were married. They were about 20 years older than me. The whole time we were out, they talked about how their friends talked badly about them. They brought up comments their friends would put on Instagram, Facebook—a lot of pointless drama. I remember sitting there, 23 years old, thinking, *Whoa, these people are quite a bit older than me and their subconscious is screaming so loudly from some deep unhappiness within. Otherwise, they wouldn't be creating this space to complain about their friends complaining about them.*

In that moment, I realized I had the opportunity to become a true Intoxicator. I recognized this energy they were spending talking about their friends was not the true issue; the true issue was something deeper. I sat there thinking, *How can I bring love into this conversation with them?* I thought, *This is my moment. This is one of my many moments to throw the starfish back into the water.* So, that is exactly what I did. I told one of my many stories, like I have told you throughout this book. I told them about the friend I mentioned in the love step, who rejected this movement, which I allowed to make me quite upset. What I told them was that before I even moved to New Zealand to follow my dream to live internationally that same friend said, "It's so frustrating that you are where you want to be, and I am not."

You see, it's not that my friend was ever rejecting the movement. It was that I was creating momentum around my dreams when my friend was not where they wanted to be yet. But since I only wanted recognition out of the conversation, both of us were trying to connect through unhealthy ways—comparison and recognition.

When I told my friends this story they were in shock, but within a moment their minds shifted and they got it. In that moment, I was an Intoxicator because I created a space to find and share the love in the situation. They could see that their friends' complaints about them were actually their friends screaming to connect with them, but they did not know how to do so in a healthy way. My friends did want to connect but felt hurt their friends could not be happy for them, so it created a connection over misunderstanding and negativity. Within that moment, I intoxicated the world with love because they could see the truth of the world; sometimes we do connect in unhealthy ways to get an instant connection because it seems much safer and easier than a deep, true connection. I threw the starfish back in and created a ripple. I will never know the result of that one starfish—that one moment I intoxicated the world with love—but at least I started by sharing the truth of the world that we all want to have love surround us.

This story is one of the many realizations as an Intoxicator. It doesn't matter your age or where you are in life, when you are looking at the world around you to give you gratification, you will never find long-term fulfilled happiness. Once you shift your mind, you'll see that who you are NEEDS to be shared into the universe because the universe needs you. You become a true Intoxicator because you see how people subconsciously find ways to remain victims. As I did in this story, I realized it was no longer about me; my shift was bigger than myself. I was doing this for the world because my life, this story, and this movement is bigger than me. It's to inspire, empower, and impact the people of the world to see all the good they can do, just by being them.

As an Intoxicator, you begin to go through life empowering people through creative ways to recognize the unworthiness they may be carrying within. You do not say these words to them, you do not even tell people you know that what they are talking about is not the real issue. All you do is find a way to bring love into the space you are sharing with others around you. As I walked through the example with my friends, I realized this conversation was not adding positivity and love into the world. I decided to actively create a place of love.

I shared with this couple my story and that the true reason their friends were "talking" about them or giving "mean" comments is because they wanted to connect but did not know how to do it in a healthy way. When I said this to my friends they were totally blown away. They did not know I was actually planting that seed of intoxicating them with love. In that moment, my friends wanted me to engage in a conversation where they were unintentionally creating a space to connect on a surface level, subconsciously masking their true desire to connect with their friends. Instead of engaging with this surface level conversation and creating a space of going in a circle about how bad the world is and how people suck, I brought love into the space. I turned a conversation going down a path of judgment and negativity into a conversation of understanding. That is the truth of an Intoxicator.

As we are now here at the Intoxicator step, this is still only the beginning of our journey. My heart was filled with so much joy when I taught myself how to become an Intoxicator and realized I bring other people in the world along on this journey too. This is only the beginning. It's only the base of the mountain for this movement. This is just our beginning. You have decided to become open to the power that you hold within, to discover all your true gifts, to courageously explore those gifts, and to unapologetically love yourself. You're going to intoxicate the world with love, with the truth of who you are to make this a better place for all of us.

INVENTING YOUR TRUTH

When I created this journey, I envisioned a life for myself where I lived in a world filled with timeless moments. It may have seemed like I was getting lost and losing touch with reality because this dream seemed too amazing to be obtainable. This movement where we inspire, empower, and impact ourselves and other people to get "lost" with being in love with life because they are courageously living their truth is just beautiful.

I am here to tell you I have not lost touch with reality, and none of the Intoxicators have lost touch with reality; we are transforming the world. The ones who have lost touch with reality are those who cannot see that courageously living their truth, intoxicating the world with love, is the only way to move this world forward. It is the only way to bring the ultimate goal of living a life with no regrets. I do not know how exactly I am going to get to my destination nor where my destination even is, but I know there is a new nation arising. This new nation is for us dreamers, visionaries, and truth seekers who know we are one, we are universal citizens, and we should be contributing to the world in this way. I know my truth, my journey, is to intoxicate the world around me to see that love is the answer; it will prevail as we grow this peaceful army.

Everything around us is only what we make of it because we attach emotion to it. Everything is just a moment, but our life is made up of a bunch of small moments. As an Intoxicator, we hold the responsibility to create moments where we empower each other to act in ways of love and understanding. We each hold a responsibility every day to ourselves, each other, and the world to live our unique truths.

As Intoxicators, we know there is something greater within each of us that we have been suppressing. It's because of the disease the world has given to us. As an Intoxicator, we begin to see all the ways we are similar and where each of us are in the Intoxicator journey. We are all trying to do our best to love and be loved, but sometimes our subconscious unworthiness will be tempted to overtake our truth. But we are aware it is part of the process, it happens. We look at ourselves and others with love and understand it is all part of the process.

As Intoxicators, we come from a place of understanding that the heavy drinking, anger, drugs, sadness, and unworthiness in others are their attempts to create a connection, but they do not know how to be vulnerable. In this step, we understand the habits, behaviors, and thoughts people carry are often within the subconscious. So as Intoxicators we are always looking for creative ways to intoxicate the world with love. Even if we never see the direct impact that a moment of love has, we know it makes a difference in the momentum of the world. We know we have a responsibility to live our truth and show the world that love is always alive. An Intoxicator is always finding ways to shine light within darkness.

In this book, I have related different snapshots from nine years of my life and how I found all the ways to not be who I truly was. This book, these five steps, and this movement can reach you wherever you are, inspiring you to shift your mindset, your behavior, and your actions to find, speak, and live your truth. This journey is realizing the power of choice you have within, the power of your unique purpose and love. I hope you have become inspired, empowered, and impacted from my story and this movement, so that you choose to start your journey of truth today.

I told my story what I've learned, and shared The Intoxicator Movement with you. My hope is that it inspires you to travel within yourself to understand there is more in life for you. When you are an Intoxicator, you not only learn to love, you inspire others around you to become motivated. You are an educator who is courageously inspiring, empowering, and impacting your truth to manifest into the world. You always hold yourself responsible to find ways to create space for people to get lost in their truth. You become an Intoxicator when it is no longer just about your true passion but the passion to serve others to show them how to get lost in the excitement of their truth.

When you become an Intoxicator, you no longer feel the need to pretend to fit into one certain education system the world puts on us. As an Intoxicator, we are the educator of ourselves in the world. We know that education is learning, it's growing, and it's ongoing. We know that knowledge is information, but information is nothing without emotion. From this journey, you understand what lights you up, and you find experts to empower you to create a plan to implement your dreams into a fulfilled and sustainable lifestyle.

As an Intoxicator, we inspire those around us to be who they are. We inspire them not to feel pressure to have to portray an amazing lifestyle while being the best mom, dad, husband, wife, aunt, sister, friend, workout guru, and so on. We inspire the world around us to realize it truly is that simple: their passion is needed in the world to increase the momentum of moving the world forward. We do not need to know it all; we learned in the love step we go to the experts for what does not light us up.

Here's a quick story about this. I still do not know very much about my cancer because I do not have interest in the medical field. I still have never read the reports the doctors wrote about my cancer. I still tell new doctors when I meet with them I cannot be bothered with the technical information of cancer because it is not my passion and it does not excite me. However, having cancer has allowed me to create a movement where I empower people to acknowledge and accept the disease given to us by the world. I have learned how to use my disease and my story to inspire, empower, and impact people to reconnect with who they are.

As an Intoxicator, we recognize people's disease, accept that we each are fighting to overcome them, and we each want to love and be loved. As I share my cancer journey, I describe my nine years of life where I created a dark room for myself, but I took my power back to overcome the darkness I created. As an Intoxicator, I hear all the awful ways the world gives us different diseases, but no matter your challenges, if you commit to being an Intoxicator, you'll live a life with no regrets. Just as I had the choice, you have the choice to start your dream today. I have created a community all over the world to start the Intoxicator roadmap to become open, to discover, to explore, to love, and to become an Intoxicator.

In this final step, we accept the responsibly to start walking around smiling at each other, instead of walking around with headphones, isolating ourselves from the world. We actively create healthy connections and empower others to connect over healthy conversations. We do not engage in blaming the world. We hold ourselves responsible to live our truth.

REALITY

no longer see negativity in the world because I do not make it my reality. All I see is the various ways people are trying to communicate to form connections. I choose only to see all the ways people are trying to connect. When I'm intoxicating the world with my love through my story, I find ways to create a safe place. I ask questions, let my guard down, and show my vulnerabilities. This creates a safe place for them to be who they are, share their love and ambitions, and bring their true passion into the world.

In this final step, you recognize all the ways people try to lock themselves in a room of darkness by placing blame on the world, as we once did. We found all the excuses of how our story, our journey, was different from everyone else's, but when you start to see all the ways other people do this, we see that we all share this tendency. As Intoxicators, we acknowledge we are all fighting a disease that has been suppressed so deeply and that we are all trying to create connection with the world around us. We are all acting in ways we think give us the greatest chance to form a connection in the world. But we know that the greatest connection, the one we crave so deeply, is only achieved by living our truth. When you begin to do this, you realize you are impacting the world to become a better place as you live your love and light with every moment you share into the world.

As an Intoxicator, we feel love very intensely and share it, but we also feel the negative emotions of life just as intensely! We need to become open to these feelings, discover why they are born, and then explore them in a healthy way to then create love with these emotions to serve this world around us. We take the moments of darkness but now feel these emotions with the intention that this dark emotion will grow our understanding of others around us. This intense emotion is empowering us to understand the various ways people's subconscious minds are trying to speak through them into the world to form a connection.

I take these moments of darkness as an opportunity to learn I no longer fight them, hold myself guilty for them, or run from them because it is just part of the process. I embrace this dark side because it motivates me to be the best Intoxicator I can be. If I can acknowledge my subconscious darkness leaking into the world trying to connect, I can then recognize it when others try to do that too. I embrace this, empowering myself to see how intoxicating others with my truth, and with love, can impact not only others but also the world. That is the truth of an Intoxicator.

OUR BEGINNING,
THE PEACEFUL ARMY OF LOVE

People ask how have I been able to transform my life to now be filled with so much positivity, energy, and love. What they are actually asking is how they too can start to attract all this positive energy and love into their own life.

I became courageous enough to release myself from the responsibility to be anyone but myself. I know that you hold the same courageous power to live your truth and attract your version of success. With this five-step process, you do not need to isolate yourself one moment longer. You can become part of this greater movement by simply being you.

You no longer need to compete with others, you no longer need to compare yourself to others, and you no longer need to get distracted by anything else except your true purpose. It is that simple. You get to choose to lose yourself in your passion and at the same time inspire, empower, and impact others to choose the path of love. By being you, you will live the fairy-tale—a fulfilling, sustainable life.

As an Intoxicator, you come from a place of understanding, love, and compassion because you know everyone is trying to create a sustainable, fulfilled life, but not everyone knows how. However, as an Intoxicator you now know it is no longer just about you. You know the world needs you as a resource, the people around you count on you, and most importantly, the world counts on you to become part of this peaceful arm of love in order for it to move forward.

This step took me nine years to learn. However, this lifestyle of becoming an Intoxicator never ends. As I am writing this book, I myself am still going through these five steps in different parts of my life that I am focusing on evolving in that moment. The journey to becoming a greater Intoxicator never stops: opening up, discovering, exploring, and loving. We continue to evolve, working with our truth and watching it evolve with us in the world.

As we grow, our hearts get bigger, our emotions become more intense, the life we craft around us will get better, and we will impact the world to be better. We start to walk through life noticing when people are giving away their power and light to external factors. We do not get angry at them, we do not get frustrated. We are able to see everyone through love, and this allows us to come from a place of understanding they are doing the best they can. They just may have not had the support around them to see how the world needs their gifts. In the Intoxicator step, get creative and intoxicate them with love so they can see it's okay to live their truth to start intoxicating the world too.

Intoxicators never stop seeking growth, we never stop creating space for others to get lost, and most importantly, we never stop loving. We live with our truth, with our love in the world. We create the space for others to join the army of love. People do not see all this great power we have within to transform the world. Our truth is realizing we do not need to fix anyone or anything—just be our truest selves to inspire others to find, speak, and live their truth. This is my favorite place because it's where we are creating the playground of our life.

I am here to tell you there is a light at the end of every dark tunnel. There is a light in every dark room, and most importantly, I acknowledge the light within you. I do not know you, but I know you are capable of the most magical things in life. I know together we are stronger than we are as individuals. I know together, with The Intoxicator Movement, you can become part of the ripple effect, just like the starfish story. Together we can create this place where we gather together as a safe place for each other to impact in the world. Together we can create the biggest universal army the world has seen, a universal nation, conquering the world through love and positivity.

This is the truth of an Intoxicator, this is my truth: a girl who overcame the disease the world gave her. This is my truth: I remained a victim for nine years of my own life. This is my truth of how I began this journey to create a life filled with endless love and positivity, so I can live the modern-day fairytale—a life with no regrets. This is the start of our truth, to travel together through love, so we can intoxicate the world together, to show the world love will prevail.

I am so happy you have joined The Intoxicator Movement. Love your truth and intoxicate the world with your truth because the world truly needs more people like you!

Until I get to meet you somewhere in the world,

Xoxo

Colleen

AUTHOR BIO

Colleen is an Intuitive, Cancer-Survivor, Podcast Host, Global Citizen, Published Author of Books, Educator, and Passionate About Empowering People to Gain Clarity On Their Purpose. She is pursuing her Ph.D. in Psychology as well.

Her most tremendous success is seeing her clients become empowered to create lifestyles that transform their lives and change the world. Colleen offers this experience through online courses, retreats, products, and social media content, so people can deepen their spiritual practices, understand the power of expression to attract opportunities, and take calculated action toward growing a sustainable impact.

Join Colleen on the journey.

www.colleengallagher.co

www.instagram.com/iamcolleengallagher

www.facebook.com/thecolleengallagher

www.twitter.com/col_gallagher1

A free ebook edition is available with the purchase of this book.

To claim your free ebook edition:

1. Visit MorganJamesBOGO.com
2. Sign your name CLEARLY in the space
3. Complete the form and submit a photo of the entire copyright page
4. You or your friend can download the ebook to your preferred device

Print & Digital Together Forever.

Snap a photo   Free ebook   Read anywhere